Seven Kings of England

Other Books by Geoffrey Trease

WEB OF TRAITORS

THE SILKEN SECRET

CUE FOR TREASON

SIR WALTER RALEIGH: *Captain and Adventurer*

THE SEVEN QUEENS OF ENGLAND

Seven Kings
of England

GEOFFREY TREASE

THE VANGUARD PRESS
NEW YORK

CONTENTS

FOREWORD

The particular seven kings in this book have been chosen for the dramatic quality in their lives and the interest (though not always the excellence) of their characters. After that I have considered variety of period: this mixed bag includes a Saxon and a Norman, a Plantagenet, a trio of Stuarts, whose reigns make three acts in one continuous play, and a "constitutional monarch" of our own century. There are no Tudors, but their family was well represented in The Seven Queens of England, *to which this book comes as a companion.*

Again I am indebted to innumerable histories and biographies that I have consulted for this fact or that, and it is only possible here to list the chief works that have helped me: Alfred the Great, The Truth Teller, *B. A. Lees;* A History of the Anglo-Saxons, *R. H. Hodgkin;* Anglo-Saxon England, *Sir Frank Stenton;* William the Conqueror, *E. A. Freeman;*

William the Conqueror, *Hilary Belloc;* Richard the Lion Heart, *K. Norgate;* Coeur de Lion, *C. A. Wilkinson;* Charles I, *Evan John;* Charles, King of England, King Charles and King Pym, *and* King Charles the Martyr, *all by E. Wingfield Stratford;* Charles II, *A. Bryant;* William III, *H. D. Traill;* George VI *and* Their Majesties, *both by Hector Bolitho;* A King's Story, *by the Duke of Windsor.*

Seven Kings of England

†

ALFRED: THE

SHEPHERD OF THE

ENGLISH

On a certain day about the middle of the ninth century, in Rome, a small English boy—he was about
four—was solemnly arrayed in the robes and ceremonial belt of a consul.

That boy was destined to become King of England. He was, in fact, to be one of the greatest who
have ever borne that title, and the first whose name is
still familiar to us. And he was, it is fairly safe to
suppose, the only Roman consul who was ever an
English king as well.

In one sense it did not mean much when Pope
Leo IV conferred the empty rank of consul on the
small boy Alfred from Wessex. It was hundreds of
years since real power had rested with Roman con-
suls such as Julius Caesar and Pompey. In the ninth
century A.D. the title was just a picturesque survival
—or revival—like the phrase "Holy Roman Em-

peror" to describe the great Frankish king Charle-magne, a generation earlier. The real Roman Empire had splintered centuries before.

But, in another sense, that ceremony in Rome did mean something.

The little boy came from an England of green woods and bare green hills. He was born in the shadow of the chalk downs at Wantage, in Berkshire, just south of Oxford, and all his childhood was spent in timber-built country manors or in miniature towns of a few thousand inhabitants, scarcely larger than the large villages of today. Such was Britain since she had ceased to be a province of the Roman empire and had been colonized by Angles and Saxons from what are now Denmark and North Germany. They were country lovers, with a spirit not unlike that of the early American pioneers, and Alfred's world was one of horses and hounds, of birds singing in the branches and fish leaping in the unsullied streams.

He had come to a city that had once held between a million and a million and a half people. The population might have fallen since the great days of the Empire, but the buildings remained. New walls had just been raised to protect the city, and those walls linked no fewer than forty-four towers. Rome was still the center and the wonder of the world under the popes. Classical ruins stood side by side with Christian churches, monasteries, and shrines. Even the most pious pilgrim gaped in wonder at the remains of the pagan amphitheater and murmured the familiar saying:

*"When falls the Colosseum, Rome shall fall,
And when Rome falls, the world."*

All his life long, Alfred was to look back upon the glories of Roman civilization as models—not just to be copied, but to be adapted to English needs. Law, learning, literature, the Latin language: those were the civilized heritage, those were what some day he was to seek for his own people.

Roman consul, King of England. . . . Memories of past greatness, foundations of greatness in the future. . . .

The little boy, smiling up at the Pope, proudly fingering his wonderful new belt, can be seen now as a link between two epochs in history.

Alfred did not talk to Leo, except through interpreters, for no pope could be expected to converse in English, and Alfred was a grown man before he managed to learn Latin.

But if Leo did put to him the usual questions that old gentlemen put to small boys, in this case with someone to translate them, he would have learned that Alfred's illustrious father, King Ethelwulf of Wessex, was well, and hoped to make the pilgrimage to Rome himself next year or the year after, if the Danish pirates did not become too active in the meantime; that Alfred was "the baby of the family," having three brothers, Ethelbald, Ethelbert, and Ethelred, and a sister, Ethelswith, who had just gone off to marry King Burhred of Mercia, the neighboring kingdom; and that the prefix "Ethel" in all the other names meant "noble" in the English tongue, but that "Alf" was the same as "elf," and meant a spirit of the earth and air.

Alfred would certainly have admitted, if he were asked, that he was proud to have been sent with this mission to Rome, in his father's name. None of his elder brothers had come.

For more detailed information, the Pope had to inquire of the priests and courtiers who formed the rest of the English party. From them, he could learn that King Ethelwulf was a mild, religious man, though he could fight bravely enough when called upon. Two years before, when the Danes had stormed London and Canterbury, he had smashed them with (as the chronicler wrote) "the greatest slaughter in the heathen army that we have ever heard tell of to this present day."

The Pope must have heard their accounts of this victory with considerable pleasure. For the Danes—or Northmen, or Norsemen, or Vikings, whatever you choose to call them, "white strangers" or "black strangers" or "heathen men"—had become the terror of Western Europe. Rome could sympathize. She had her own similar problem, the Saracens, or Moors as they were named in Spain. Their galleys swept the Mediterranean just as the Danish long ships swept the outer ocean. Only nine years before, the Saracens had landed near Rome herself, looting churches and defiling the very tombs of the Apostles.

Any success against the heathen, whether Dane or Saracen, came as a crumb of comfort.

How strong was King Ethelwulf? Was he the effec-

tive overlord of all England, the "Bretwalda," as *his*
father, King Egbert, had been? Or was he just the
ruler of the West Saxons?

The Pope knew that England was divided into
several Saxon kingdoms and that the Welsh still held
the mountainous westerly corners, Cornwall and
Wales and the Lake District. The chief Saxon kingdoms were Wessex in the south (the name is a con-
traction of "West Saxons"), Mercia in the middle, and Northumbria in the northeast. Each in turn,
starting with Northumbria, had had its age of greatness, when it had taken the lead and its kings had
been looked up to as overlords by their neighbors.
The turn of Wessex had come last. Alfred's grandfather had ruled Mercia as well as his own realm; he
had been virtually king of all England south of the
Humber, the deep-cut river mouth that indents the
northeast coast and makes one of the great natural
divisions of the country.

No, the Englishmen told Leo, Ethelwulf was a less
ambitious man than Egbert. He was satisfied with
Wessex, which meant only England south of the
Thames, plus Essex to the north (but not London),
and minus Cornwall in the far west. But he kept up
the closest friendship with the Mercians and had
given his daughter in marriage to their king.

But it was no small thing to be king of only Wessex. The Pope would see for himself, when Ethelwulf
paid his long-looked-for visit to the holy city.

Leo did not live to see, but his successor did. When
Alfred returned to Rome two years later, eager to
point out its wonders to his father, the old gentleman

who had given him the consular belt was no more. A new Pope had just been elected, Benedict III, and it was to him that Ethelwulf and Alfred had to offer the splendid gifts they had brought with them. A crown of pure gold, a gold-chased sword, a gold-embroidered tunic, golden chalices for the altar, silver-gilt hanging lamps of the finest English craftsmanship, delicately woven materials. . . . England was no longer an outlying, barbarous island on the fringe of the world, as she had seemed to the earlier Romans. She was among the richest and most civilized countries in Christendom.

In case any of the Roman nobility and clergy should have any doubt on this point, the new Pope advised Ethelwulf to be generous. The English king took the hint. Gold coins were distributed lavishly, and even the common people received silver. Smiles greeted the fair-skinned pilgrims wherever they went.

This time Alfred spent a whole year in Rome, and he was old enough to understand and remember much more than on his first visit. His mother, Osburh, had died a little while before they left home. Both the King and his little son were glad to forget their grief, as far as they could, among the strange sights of this far-off capital. None of the other boys had come. The eldest, in fact, was ruling Wessex on his father's behalf. Alfred, as the youngest, had always had a rather special place in his parents' affection.

He was one of the few Saxon princes to have seen Rome. Almost certainly, no boy of his rank had ever spent so long there. And what a change it was, after the wandering country life at home!

For, at home in England, like an old-fashioned company of strolling players, his father's court was forever on the move. It had to be. There were no towns big enough to feed it for more than a few weeks at a time. A king had to move from one royal estate to another, using up the provisions due him from the local farms, and then pass on. Also, to insure that the country was properly governed and justice done, he had to supervise everything in person.

In babyhood Alfred had known the jingle of harness and the clop of hoofs as his lullaby. The sway of a wagon or the ambling gait of a quiet horse had rocked him as often as an indoor cradle. From the first opening of his eyes he had known the slow march of overhanging forest branches against the sky behind, and, as he had grown old enough to sit up, the view had merely changed to that of a road, stretching endlessly ahead, with the backs of jogging horsemen in the foreground. Dust and sun, mud, rain, and snow, biting winds, mist, and frost—he had known them all, as traveling companions, ever since he could remember. The two long journeys to Rome, across France and down half the length of Italy, had meant no fresh hardship, only a change of view.

It was Rome itself that was the great change: paved streets, mighty girdling walls and towers, churches and palaces, splendid processions and services, wise and holy men reading out of books, and worldly, traveled men, with tales of far southern and eastern countries.

Even as a boy, Alfred was deeply religious. Perhaps, in those early days, there were some who thought he would become a priest. With all those elder brothers, he was not likely to be needed as a ruler. And there could not be much of an inheritance awaiting him as the youngest of the King's sons.

Yet, somehow, those who knew Alfred best could scarcely imagine him in some quiet cloister. There was another side to the boy's character. He loved tales of adventure—whether they were the old poems and stories of his Saxon forefathers or new, firsthand yarns spun by sea captains and wandering traders. He loved all songs and music, not only the chants of the Church. And he loved sport and looked forward to the day when he would be old enough to ride with his brothers after the red deer.

He meant to fight the Danes, too, if they came back. He had been too young to go with his father and eldest brother when they went off to beat the invaders in 851—it was even hard to be sure now whether he actually remembered their triumphant homecoming or whether he only imagined he did, having heard the story so often told and retold. He had been so very little at the time.

Would the Danes come back?

Some people said no, they had learned their lesson. Others said the Danes always came back. Some said the Danes were God's punishment for the wickedness of England. Father hoped that England had been punished enough by now, and that by coming on this pilgrimage to Rome in person, and making

all these rich offerings at St. Peter's, he had earned
God's forgiveness for his people. The worldlier men
in Rome smiled sadly when they heard this argument. England was not the only country that suffered
from these northern invaders. Nothing seemed to
stop them.

They came buzzing out of Scandinavia like wasps,
out of the sandy Danish creeks and the rocky Nor-
wegian fiords. It was only partly the love of piracy
that drove them; it was also sheer necessity. As the
population increased, the northern countries could
not support it. There was just not enough farmland.
Some of the people had to move out or starve.

It was certainly true that other countries in Western Europe had suffered at least as heavily as England. Not long before this time Rouen, Nantes, and
Hamburg had been plundered, Paris and Bordeaux
besieged. The dreaded long ships had been seen as
far south as Spain. They had rowed up the Guadal-
quivir as far as Seville—that was always their way, to
use the rivers to strike at the heart of a country—
but at Seville they had been beaten back by the Saracens. One scourge of Christendom had clashed with
the other. To the Saxons it seemed a pity the heathen
did not meet more often to exterminate each other!

At last the long year in Rome came to an end, and
the English party turned their horses' heads northwards. Ethelwulf seemed in no hurry to go home.
They spent several months at the court of King
Charles of the West Franks. He was the grandson of
the mighty emperor Charlemagne and had inherited
a share of his empire, the westerly French portion.

There had long been a friendship between the French and the English—wars between them were still far in the future—and there were old men who could remember Alfred's grandfather as a guest at Charlemagne's court, before he became King of Wessex.

King Charles had a daughter Judith. She was twelve or thirteen, twice as old as Alfred, to whom she seemed almost grown up. Nonetheless, it came as rather a surprise when he learned that she was going to be married to his father. He wondered how his elder brothers would feel when his father brought them home a stepmother. The wedding took place at the end of the summer. It was the Archbishop of Rheims who married the middle-aged king to the girl-princess. After the usual festivities, the English party set out on the last stage of their homeward journey.

What Alfred thought of it all we do not know. But Wessex disliked the marriage exceedingly, and Ethelbald, who had been left to rule the country during his father's absence, plotted to prevent his return and to usurp the throne. Civil war was barely avoided. Ethelwulf forgave his son, and for the short remaining period of his life he shared the government with him.

Ethelwulf died when Alfred was nine. Ethelbald then became unchallenged king—and promptly caused a considerable scandal by marrying his father's widow (his own stepmother), who was still in her teens. Within two years Ethelbald himself died, and his next brother, Ethelbert, became king. The interesting Judith then retired to her native country and disappears from English history, though not entirely without trace. It is thought that Alfred as a boy may have picked up from her, or one of her Frankish attendants, the germ of the idea that grew into that unique historical record, the *Anglo-Saxon Chronicle,* after he became king.

One more fact about this young lady may be worth mentioning: despite the upsets caused by her first two marriages, she proceeded to shock her own family by running off with Baldwin of the Iron Arm, Count of Flanders. The iron arm seems to have been strong enough to restrain her from any further wanderings.

Meanwhile, as she sailed away from England and Alfred's next brother mounted the throne, the Danes burst into Wessex and were not driven out until they had plundered Winchester, just north of the modern port of Southampton. It is scarcely surprising that, as Alfred complained in later years, his education was neglected when he was a boy.

It was as though a curse brooded over the royal family of Wessex—and in those days men really believed in curses.

One by one Ethelwulf's sons were dying. The second, Ethelbert, reigned only five or six years. He was followed by Ethelred. Alfred was now seventeen, and though Ethelred was married and had baby sons, he was next in line to the throne until those sons should grow to manhood. In such troubled times only a grown fighting man was fit to wear a crown. Not for some centuries would it be handed on, by the strict rule of "primogeniture," to the first-born son of the previous king.

Life was uncertain, quite apart from the risks of battle. Fond though Alfred was of sport and exercise, his health was not good. Some ailment (we do not know what) dogged him through his teens, and another illness, more serious but equally unknown, came upon him at nineteen and afflicted him off and on for the rest of his life. All we know is that it brought him bouts of agonizing pain, with long spells of depression between. Again, there were those who believed that he had been cursed by someone with the evil eye.

This mysterious ailment first struck him on his wedding day. For, at nineteen, he married Ealswith, a girl of royal blood from Mercia, the Saxon Kingdom to the north of Wessex.

What Ealswith looked like—or was like—is unknown. But it seems to have been a happy enough marriage, lasting all Alfred's life (she died shortly after him) and blessed with children.

What is more surprising is that we do not know what Alfred himself looked like. No statue or portrait survives, no clear description in words. If the roughly stamped faces on his coins are meant as a likeness, they merely tell us that he was clean-shaven. The bearded figure that stands in the market place of Wantage, his native town, is based on pure guesswork, like all other statues and pictures supposed to represent him.

There are, in fact, a great many facts about Alfred

we are never likely to know. His birthday. How, and exactly when, he died. Did he really burn the cakes when he was hiding from the Danes? And did he disguise himself as a harper and venture into their camp as a spy? We might as well clear these points out of the way at once and admit our ignorance. They are interesting but of minor importance. In other, more vital, ways we can know Alfred more vividly than most of the public figures in today's newspaper.

That summer of his marriage to Ealswith, there was a crisis in the affairs of England.

The period of mere raids was over: the Danish invasion of England had begun in earnest.

Two or three years before, the Danes had landed in East Anglia, and, instead of sailing away again after the usual campaign in search of plunder, had moved inland and northwards into Yorkshire. There, after a tremendous battle and massacre at York itself, they had crushed the once-proud kingdom of Northumbria and destroyed it as a fighting force.

They were now firmly established in northern England. Not satisfied with this, within two years they were riding down into the Midlands, to join another army that sailed up the River Trent in long ships. The two forces met at Nottingham (later famous as the town of Robin Hood), where they entrenched themselves in a great palisaded camp, with the broad stream in front and the dense oak woods of Sherwood at their backs.

Mercia mobilized to meet the danger. Minor raids could often be dealt with by a king and his own household troops, consisting of his thanes or noblemen and their own sworn followers. But to meet a big attack he would call out the *fyrd,* or general levy of fighting men, each armed and equipped according to his class—the poor peasant with spear and shield, the richer man with three-foot sword or battle-ax, mail shirt, and helmet of iron and horn. Bows and arrows were not used much, but at close quarters both spears and axes were sometimes thrown.

Messengers were sent to King Ethelred to ask for help from Wessex. Ethelred called out his own *fyrd* and marched to join the Mercians in front of the Danish camp at Nottingham, a hundred miles north of his own borders. Alfred left his new bride, donned helmet and mail shirt, and rode with his brother.

It was his first sight of the Danes, who were to be his lifelong enemies.

There, beneath the earthen banks and stockade of the camp, lay the hated long ships—clinker-built, oaken vessels, graceful and cruel of line, nearly eighty feet from carved beak to rudder post. They had sixteen rowers to a side and one square sail. These were the craft that had made the heathen men masters not only of every sea and coast but of every inland place that could be reached by river. "Ravens of the wind," the Danes called them, "reindeers of the breezes," and "horses of the gull's track."

And there, too, moving about on the riverside, were the heathen men themselves, with their barbaric-looking helmets, winged or horned, and their long beards and mustaches. Their equipment was the finest in the world. Unlike the conscripted peasants of the *fyrd,* even the Danish rank and file were plentifully supplied with mail shirts. Their terrible battle-axes were developed from the lumber axes they used daily in the forests at home. Their spears were strong, their swords well balanced by heavy pommels, which gave extra protection to the metal guard of the hilt.

Alfred's brother and brother-in-law, the Mercian king, had to decide whether or not to attack the camp, for the Danes showed no signs of venturing into the open. It was a hard decision. In one way it was a pity to miss the chance of a combined blow, now that the Wessex men had marched so far from their own country. But—what if the blow failed? No one had ever stormed a Danish camp successfully. Suppose the attack ended in disaster, and the Danes, sallying forth, smashed the wavering ranks of the Saxons? Then not only the north of England, but the whole of England, might be lost forever.

The Wessex men, having come so far, favored taking a chance. It was the Mercians, according to a later chronicler, who "made peace with the host," that is, the Danish horde. Alfred saw only a few light skirmishes before a treaty was made. Then he rode home with his people, while the Mercians collected the *geld,* or ransom, with which the invaders were to be bought off. Only when it was safely handed over did the Danes retire to Northumbria. They always kept their word—for the time being.

But, even back in Wessex, Alfred could not fail to be aware of the doom creeping over the island. Messengers and refugees brought the news, month by month. Bought off by Mercia, the heathen tide was flowing back over East Anglia. And by New Year, 871—Alfred's "year of battles" as it came to be called —the winged helmets were on the Thames at Reading, prepared to sweep forward into Wessex.

It was here that the chalk ridges of the Chiltern Hills faced, across the river, that other ridge of the Berkshire Downs that went slanting away into the heart of Wessex. The dry chalk, with its ancient skyline track raised high above swamp and forest, offered the perfect invasion route for a land army.

As at Nottingham, the Danes entrenched themselves by the river. The local Saxons mustered under the elderman—or "alderman," to give the title in its modern spelling—and defeated one band of raiders, driving them back to their camp. Meanwhile Ethelred and his young brother were gathering the main army of mid-Wessex. There was no time to get help from the far west, and they marched on Reading with what forces they had. The Danish outposts fell back before them. Gaining confidence, Ethelred and Alfred did what the Mercians had not dared to do at Nottingham: they swept boldly up to the Danish ramparts. They learned, then, that perhaps the cautious Mercians had been right after all. For, as the chronicler says, "the heathen themselves fought with valor, and rushing out of all the gates like wolves, joined battle with all their might. There for a long time both sides fought fiercely, but alas! the Christians at last turned their backs and the heathen gained the victory. . . ."

Alfred and his brother fell back along the Berk-

shire Downs, rallying their forces as best they could.
The war was not lost. Fresh contingents of Saxons
were riding hard to join their king. The Danes made
the mistake of not following up their victory. They
settled down to an orgy of deep drinking, while,
not twenty miles away, the Saxons recovered their
strength for a counterblow.

Ethelred did not expect the Danes to follow him
at all just at present, for he fixed his camp beneath
Lowbury Hill, whereas the nearby Louse Hill
(known to this day by the gypsies as "the Hill of
Destruction") would have been a stronger position.
So when the Danes did move out in pursuit of their
enemy, after their two or three days of merrymaking,
they were able to occupy this higher ground themselves. They got there at dusk on January 7, and all
through that long winter night the two armies lay
within a thousand yards of each other.

Dawn came. The Danes could be seen forming
two columns, one on either side of the ancient track-
way. From the banners it could be seen that two
Danish kings were to head one column, while their
earls led the other. Ethelred held a council of war,
and it was decided to form two columns to meet
them. He himself would attack the kings, Alfred
would charge the earls. It did not occur to Ethelred
that the Danes might do the attacking: it was their
custom to occupy a strong position, such as a fort or
some higher ground, as in this case, and there await
their enemies. Ethelred was so sure that the Danes
would wait that he gave orders for Mass to be celebrated in his tent.

A few minutes later the Danish kings gave the word, and both enemy columns began to pour down the slope, blowing their horns, clashing their arms, and raising a bloodcurdling chorus.

Alfred and his thanes stood for a moment aghast. The Danes were now only half a mile away, coming down into the hollow between the two hills where a single thorn tree stood out as a gaunt landmark. On open ground such as this, the attacker had the advantage—the armed man, charging the last yards at full tilt, was more likely to overthrow an opponent who merely stood still and waited for him. It was not only a physical question but a psychological one, too.

There was no time to ask King Ethelred, still kneeling before the little altar set up in his tent. Alfred had to act on his own. He made a quick decision and ordered his men to charge, leading them "like a wild boar," wrote Bishop Asser, the friend who afterwards wrote Alfred's biography. Alfred's column moved forward, keeping shoulder to shoulder, locking their shields edge to edge in an overlapping "shield wall," as far as their speed and the roughness of the ground allowed them. And Ethelred came out of his tent to see his own half of the Saxon army advancing parallel with his young brother's.

The two pairs of columns crashed head on in the low ground between the two hilltops. The shield walls quivered, were broken here and there, knit together again. The Danes reeled from the shock and gave ground a little. Swords and axes rose and fell in the pale January light. The hottest struggles raged around the banners of the leaders, and amid all stood the solitary tree, the naked thorn.

One of the two Danish kings went down. So did five of their foremost earls and countless numbers of their fighting men. To this day the gypsies call that dip between the hills "Awful Bottom," and just to the east of it they speak of "Dead Man's Hollow."

The Danes broke and fled, back along the ridge to the safety of their entrenchments at Reading. Alfred and his men kept up the pursuit until nightfall. From that day the Saxons knew—and the Danes knew, too—that it was possible for the heathen host to be beaten in fair fight.

This was the Battle of Ashdown, and it was only the first in that year of battles. We are not sure even where they were fought: indeed, experts argue about the site of Ashdown itself. The results were doubtful, too. In spite of the Saxon triumph at Ashdown and their hard fighting in later engagements, the end of the year found the Danes still prowling, wolflike, on the threshold of Wessex. But something happened more far-reaching in its results than any of the battles. In May, Ethelred died. His two sons were too young to rule. Alfred became king, elected by the *witan,* or council, and "with the full consent of all the inhabitants of the kingdom."

It was a war-worn little country he took over. By the end of that year the fighting men of Wessex were exhausted. But the Danes, too, for the moment had had enough. Alfred made a treaty with them. He paid them to go away, back into those northern and midland regions, where they were now firmly established. It was not a glorious ending to the "year of battles" that had opened with the victory of Ashdown, but there was nothing else to do.

At least the Danes stayed away, and the young king, still in his early twenties, had a few years of peace. Burned homes and churches could be rebuilt, neglected land could be brought into better order, flocks and herds could be raised to their full numbers. Something perhaps could be done about the decline in education and culture that must have been developing over a long period, and which could not be blamed upon the invaders.

The monasteries, which served as the schools, the universities, and the publishing houses of those days, were no longer attracting first-class men and women in great numbers. And Wessex, which best withstood the Danes, seemed worse off in culture and education than those more northerly regions where the heathen had struck hardest. As Alfred wrote in later years to the Bishop of Worcester, in Mercia, "It has often come into my remembrance what wise men there formerly were among the English race, and how foreigners came to this land for wisdom and instruction." But now, he went on, there was such a decline that it was the turn of the foreigners to come and teach the English. Few men could read their prayer books even in their own language, and hardly any could translate a letter written in Latin.

Without Latin, Alfred knew, there could be no easy contact with Rome and the other courts of Christendom, no understanding of the Scriptures and

other books in which the wisdom of former generations was preserved.

Education, however, was a slow process. Dear
though it was to his heart, there was not much he
could do in the first years of his reign.

Meanwhile he grappled with the day-to-day problems of governing and enjoyed a happy family life
with Ealswith. Children came: first a girl, Ethelflaed,
then a boy Edward, destined to carry on the royal
line. In all, Alfred was to have three sons, of whom
one died young, and three daughters.

The Danes busied themselves elsewhere. They always followed the line of least resistance. They had
turned to England, for on the whole it had offered
more loot and less organized resistance than either
Ireland, France, or Spain at that time. And in England they were leaving Wessex, the toughest foe, until
the end. Northumbria they had smashed at York;
East Anglia was too small a region to offer much resistance; Mercia, weak-spirited, had become a "col-
laborator"—Alfred's brother-in-law, King Burhred,
retired to Rome, and the Danes set up a Saxon puppet ruler to act under their orders.

The Danes were nearly ready to take their last
bite.

Alfred had been king for about four years when
the heathen wolf pack snapped again at Wessex—
but failed to get their teeth into a vital spot.

The Danes broke through to Wareham, in Dorset,
and then to Exeter, farther along the south coast.
Alfred fought them on land and sea. The war lasted
a year or two in all, and was ended by a stroke of

luck. The Danish fleet was wrecked off the Dorset coast, near Swanage. One hundred and twenty long ships were destroyed in the storm, with untold casualties. Each vessel held about fifty men. Some of the six thousand, despite the weight of mail shirts and armlets, may have struggled ashore or been picked up by their comrades. At all events, the disaster was so great that the Danes hurriedly made peace, offered Alfred as many hostages as he liked, and withdrew their army into Mercia.

It was a merry Christmas that year in Wessex. More than for many long years past, it must have been a season of hope. Church and cathedral echoed with exultant music as the Saxons celebrated the birth of the Child Christ and the assurance of God's love for men that it implied. Was not the storm at Swanage a proof that God would deliver the Christian from the heathen? And when High Mass gave place to feasting in the halls, and feasting in turn gave place to singing and storytelling, what a moment to recall old times and bygone victories, to shake the oaken rafters with thunderous laughter and song!

Christmas was a leisurely festival, extending over twelve days—for what were twelve days when the daylight was at its shortest, the land probably too frozen or too flooded for work, and the stock reduced to a minimum, because of the shortage of winter feed? Christmas was a time to rest, relax, and rejoice, and to dream of spring.

The Danes waited until the end of the festival period, Twelfth Night, and then they struck.

Their leader was a king named Guthrum, who had led the invasion into Dorset a year or two before. The losses at Swanage had been made good, for the Danes were continually getting reinforcements, either from home or from their other armies. They had a loose but convenient organization. Groups were banded together under leaders, with an arrangement to share their plunder; these groups in turn combined to form armies, perhaps only for a single campaign. And there might be an even looser kind of cooperation between armies and fleets a great distance apart.

Guthrum, for instance, seems to have had an understanding with another Danish commander whose army spent that winter in South Wales. Suppose these other Danes crossed the Bristol Channel and landed in North Devon? Suppose the "Welshmen" of Cornwall, who had no love for the Saxons, could be used as allies to make trouble in the far west? And suppose Guthrum himself, then at Gloucester, made a surprise thrust into Wiltshire and down into Hampshire? The long, narrow kingdom of Wessex would be cut through the middle from the Thames to the English Channel. The western half, still rich and most of it never before touched by Danish raids, would be crushed between Guthrum and his allies in Devon and Cornwall. The easterly half could be rolled up at leisure, later on.

It was a masterly plan, and it began with a master stroke.

Guthrum gathered his men, made a surprise march, and pounced on Chippenham, a little town beside the Wiltshire Avon. It is not certain whether Alfred was there at the time. Usually the royal family spent Christmas at Dorchester, but one of the King's estates *was* at Chippenham, and it had been the place chosen, long before, for the marriage of his sister to the Mercian king. So it might well have been honored with Alfred's presence for the festival.

Wherever Alfred was, he was taken off guard. There was no time to call out the *fyrd*. With his thanes and household troops, he fell back into the woods and swamps of Somerset. Not—as the old stories suggest—as a desperate fugitive, alone and helpless. He had men with him, and all the resources of West Somerset and Devon to back him. The swamps, which were later to be known as Sedgemoor and give their name to another historic campaign, guarded the gap between two walls of hills, the Quantocks and the Blackdowns. Lurking there with a small force, Alfred could bar Guthrum's path if he chose to move westwards toward that gap. If Guthrum moved south toward Winchester and the English Channel, Alfred was still a threat to his flank.

Guthrum must have known this. Though his raiders thrust on into Hampshire, spreading panic there and driving the more frightened inhabitants overseas, he himself spent the rest of the winter near Chippenham.

He realized that there was still Alfred to be dealt with.

Sedgemoor is really sedge-meer ("sedge" meaning marsh grasses, and "mere" swampy pool)—not a moor at all, that is, but a vast expanse of flat land, in those days continually flooded by its rivers or the nearby sea. Only in modern times have embankments and drains turned it into farmland. Its homesteads and hamlets still stand, as they have stood for centuries, on the knobs and patches of higher ground, which every few years, when there are especially bad floods, become again the islets they were in Alfred's day. It is easy then to imagine the scene as it once was. One has only to blot out, in the mind's eye, the fences and telegraph poles and other modern objects that stand out of the leaden water, substitute reeds, and clothe the higher ground with trees and undergrowth. The horizon is unchanged—eastwards the gray wall of the Mendips, southwards the Blackdowns, westwards the gracefully dipping wave of the Quantocks. Unchanged, too, are the island silhouettes—the long, low outline of the tiny Polden range, the shark fin of Glastonbury Tor, King Arthur's Avalon. And, while thinking of Alfred, it is hard not to remember Arthur, too. Surely Tennyson had this landscape in mind when he wrote *Morte d'Arthur?*

> *"On one side lay the Ocean, and on one*
> *Lay a great water, and the moon was full. . . ."*

And:

> *"I heard the water lapping on the crag,*
> *And the long ripple washing in the reeds. . . ."*

Into these fenland fastnesses Alfred and his small force retreated to gather their strength again. Life was rough, but they were neither friendless nor starving. Some of the nearby villages were royal manors; any of the others would, in such an emergency, spare the King what they could from their limited winter stores. But it *was* winter, in one of the dampest, coldest spots imaginable, and they were fighting a guerrilla campaign. Probably no other English king has ever lived so hard, at least within his own realm.

It was only for a few months, however, not for several years as the old stories relate.

Through January, February, and most of March, Alfred was continually on the move. Then, about Easter, which fell that year on March 23, there came great news from the west: the thanes of Devon had smashed the other Danish army that had invaded them from South Wales. The Danish king was dead, his famous Raven banner captured, his force almost annihilated. And with those Danes died any hope of stirring up the Cornishmen to stab the Saxons in the back. The pincer movement had failed: Alfred had only the one enemy, Guthrum, to deal with.

This was the moment when he established his famous fort on the island of Athelney and intensified his raids against the Danes.

Athelney covered a mere twenty-four acres of ground, raised thirty or forty feet above the general level of the fens. Writing three hundred years later, when it could not have changed much, William of Malmesbury, a monkish historian and himself a Somerset man, wrote that it was ". . . not an island of the sea, but so cut off by flooded marshes and bogs that it can only be reached by boat." Athelney was densely clothed with alders, which gave shelter to deer and other game.

Huts were built, and no doubt a stockade, but Alfred had no intention of staying there for long. Messengers were sent out. The scattered fighting men of Wiltshire and Hampshire were bidden to prepare for the great day. The King was coming back to them, out of the west, bringing with him the fresh and untouched levies of Somerset. They were to meet at Egbert's Stone, a landmark on high ground at the junction of the three shires, as the Saxons called their counties. The place lay in Selwood, one of the vast English forests, that has long been only a dim memory.

The day fixed was in mid-May. For hours the different bands came trooping in, some mounted, some on foot, their newly burnished arms twinkling in the sunlight that filtered through the young leaves. Alfred rode in from Athelney, and the oaken aisles of the forests must have echoed with his soldiers' welcome, for they saw him "as one restored to life after many tribulations."

It was a short campaign. One day's march, one more night in camp, and then battle.

The fight took place at Ethandun, probably the modern Edington, on the chalk downs of Wiltshire. Guthrum's whole army was mustered, and the struggle was fierce and long. But Alfred's advancing shield wall held firm. At last the Danes turned and fled for the safety of their camp at Chippenham. The Saxons

remounted—for even the horsemen fought on foot
—and galloped on their heels, cutting down all the
fugitives they could.

For two weeks Alfred besieged Guthrum at Chippenham. Then the Danes surrendered, a treaty was
made, and after three weeks Guthrum was baptized
a Christian. Alfred himself stood godfather to his
enemy.

The great victory of Ethandun was not, unfortunately, the end of Alfred's struggle with the Danes.

Even Guthrum was to break his word and slip
back into his old ways until, after a second sharp
lesson, he settled down under his new Christian
name, Athelstan, as King of East Anglia. Nor were
other Danish adventurers bound by Guthrum's
promises. To the very end of his life Alfred had still
to reckon with Danish invasions, as did his son and
grandson after him, but the dark days of Athelney
were never to return.

Alfred's agreement with Guthrum left the Danes
holding the eastern counties, but their puppet ruler
disappeared from Mercia and that onetime independent kingdom came under the overlordship of
Wessex again. Alfred's eldest daughter married the
elderman, Ethelred, and herself bore the title Lady
of the Mercians, but there was no question that
Alfred was now King of England, except for the
Danish-occupied territory. His second daughter in
due time became Abbess of Shaftesbury, and the
youngest, Alfthryth, married Baldwin II, Count of

Flanders, son of the romantic Judith who had once run away with Iron Arm.

Alfred's first concern was to strengthen the defenses of his enlarged kingdom. Long before, in Spain, the Saracens had shown that ships were the best safeguard against pirates. Alfred took note. He had already gone to sea against his enemies, and now he became the founder of the first regular English navy. Progress was gradual, but toward the end of his reign he commissioned new and bigger warships to his own designs. They were about twice as long as the Danish vessels and carried sixty oars. He brought shipbuilders over from Frisia (now part of Holland) and stiffened his navy with volunteers from that country.

But in that age of oars and clumsy sails and lack of radio communication, raiders might always slip through defenses. So Alfred established fortified towns or boroughs to hold his frontiers and coasts and to command key points on the rivers up which the enemy might sail. The labor and expense caused a good deal of murmuring among the people, for not every Saxon had learned from the Danes, as the King had, what a vital part such strong points could play. Altogether, Alfred founded or refounded about twenty-five towns.

One other lesson he had absorbed: the Dane, as a full-time professional fighter, always had the advantage over the Saxon conscript, who had half his mind on the neglected fields at home. Alfred could not afford a big standing army, but he lightened the burden as much as he could. The *fyrd* was divided into two groups, only one of which was liable to duty at a given time.

Having cleared his realm of enemies and barred the door against them, Alfred was able at last to set his house in order.

The turmoil of the Danish wars—the burning of property and records, the ebb and flow of refugees, the looting and general scattering of possessions —had spread confusion everywhere, tempting and assisting thieves and criminals of all types. The general decay of religion added to the immorality and lawlessness.

Alfred set out to restore law and order. He could not point to a row of printed volumes: unwritten custom was a big element in Saxon behavior, there were no Acts of Parliament, and custom varied locally. Alfred is remembered as "the lawgiver," but he did not dictate a whole code of new rules of his own. More tactfully, he had the old laws collected, written down, and published, even though in some cases—dating from different times and districts—they might seem to contradict one another. The main thing was that in the future people would have something in black and white to guide them. If they interpreted these in the light of Christianity and local custom, they would not go far wrong.

"In the light of Christianity . . ." Alfred knew that mere laws and punishments would not ensure a decent national life, yet the Church could be of little use until its standards were raised, especially its standards of scholarship.

He summoned to his court all the men of learning he could attract. It is clear that Wessex had fallen to a low level educationally, because most of these scholars came from other regions.

Asser, who came unwillingly at first but remained as a stanch admirer of Alfred and wrote his biography, was a Welshman. There were several Mercians, Grimbald from France, John the Old Saxon (that is, from the original Saxon homeland in Germany), John the Scot, and others.

Feeling that the wisdom and knowledge of the past were enshrined in Latin, the common language of all Christian scholars, Alfred lamented the decline of Latin in his own kingdom. But, while doing all he could to restore it, he was determined to open the doors of learning to a wider public. He wished to see "all the freeborn youth of England set to learning until they can well read English writing." He founded a school at court, where the youngest of his own sons studied with other children of noble birth, so that in later years England had what no other western country possessed—a ruling class of laymen who could read. He stimulated learning everywhere. It is reckoned that nearly half his revenue was spent, in one way or another, on educational purposes. One feels sad that one cannot believe the legend that he founded University College, Oxford—though it seems true enough that he founded Oxford as a town.

Alfred was not content to wait until the next generation grew up to take over the government. He tackled their fathers on the spot. Aldermen and other officials were given strong hints that they had better learn to read if they hoped to continue in positions of responsibility. Old men went to their lessons. Alfred set the example. He was never too proud to learn. Though he could read and write his own language, he found Latin as stiff an obstacle as any modern schoolboy has ever done. But he ground away at it as doggedly as he had fought the Danes.

Latin, he realized, was not for everybody. The rest must be satisfied with reading English—but what *was* there for them to read? So he embarked on another ambitious task, the translation into English of the best Latin books he knew. It must be realized that Alfred's English was very different from our own language, and much closer to Dutch and German. Students today have to learn it as a foreign language.

Alfred chose parts of the Bible, and books on theology, philosophy, history, and geography by such men as Bede and Boethius, Orosius and Gregory. Where necessary, he adapted and modernized the text to make it clear to English readers. Much of what we know about his character is deduced from these personal touches. He did a great deal of the translation himself, but he had help from Asser, from Werferth, Bishop of Worcester, and from other friends.

Once, when he was talking to Asser, he was struck by a certain passage in a book they were discussing. Pulling out a little prayer book from the folds of his tunic, he asked Asser to copy the quotation into the margin. Asser could not find enough room, so he took a clean quire of parchment, saying that there might be other extracts to copy down later. There were. In time the eight leaves of the original quire grew into a whole volume of quotations—*flosculos,* or "little flowers," culled from the Gospels or whatever Alfred happened to be reading. They called the book by the Greek name of *Encheiridion,* that is, a "handbook" or "manual," and Alfred kept it by him night and day.

One of Alfred's greatest literary works was his foundation of the *Anglo-Saxon Chronicle,* a national record instead of a mere local one such as various monasteries had kept before. It is thought that he took the idea from the West Franks. It is a history of varying quality and value (the early parts, dealing with events outside living memory, are naturally less reliable), but it was continued right into the twelfth century. Alfred either wrote or supervised the part compiled in his own lifetime, but it was never used to glorify his own actions, as it would have been by most monarchs.

Truth teller, lawgiver, England's darling, shepherd of the English—these are some of the descriptions given to Alfred by those who knew him or who came soon after him. It was not until the seventeenth century that any writer spoke of him as "the Great."

One quality that must have struck his friends was his self-discipline. Racked by pain, haunted by depression, beset by public cares, Alfred never gave in. There was so much to do, so much to learn. Having no clock, he measured his days by candles, inventing a horn lantern to make sure they burned evenly. Not a minute was wasted. He would deliver judgment in a law case while he washed his hands. There must be time for reading and translation, time for exercise, for talk with learned friends or with sea captains who had sailed the polar seas, time for a warm and affectionate family life, time to invest his little grandson Athelstan, at an unusually early age, with the scarlet cloak, jeweled belt, and sword in a golden scabbard that betokened a royal thane.

Alfred died in his early fifties. *"So long as I have lived,"* he had written, *"I have striven to live worthily. I desire to leave the men who come after me a remembrance in good works."* There was no doubt he had succeeded. He had left his people a legacy that cannot be measured.

One day, in that darkest of his winters, he lost an ornament, a small jewel, not far from Athelney. It was found more than eight hundred years later, and today it lies in the Ashmolean Museum at Oxford. It is a fine example of Anglo-Saxon art, carried out in gold, enamel, and rock crystal. It shows a tiny figure, and around the curved edge run these words:

AELFRED MEC HEHT GEWYRCAN

"Alfred had me made . . ."

Not only the little jewel, but England herself might have said that.

THE YEARS BETWEEN

901-1026

In the century and a quarter between the death of Alfred and the birth of William the Conqueror, ordinary life in England did not change greatly. Wars continued. The Danes could never be dislodged from the eastern counties of England called the "Danelaw," but, on the other hand, they never managed to conquer the rest of the country. Gradually Saxon and Dane learned to live as neighbors, and soon, by intermarriage, as kinsmen. They were not so far removed in stock and language that they could not develop a sense of unity. There was one moment, just before William the Conqueror was born, when it looked as though this newly mixed nation might become just one dominion of a Scandinavian empire. That was in 1018, when Canute, besides being accepted as King of England, was also ruler of Norway and Denmark. But the moment passed. Canute's sons could not hold their inheritance to-

gether, and the Godwins of Wessex brought back the old Saxon royal line with Edward the Confessor. England remained an island apart, firmly English, her kings leaders rather than despots, wearing the crown with the agreement of their nobles rather than by absolute right of inheritance.

Men plowed their fields as they had done in Alfred's time. The towns might be a little bigger, but not much. Little monasteries and nunneries kept the light of religion and scholarship alive, but the whole tempo was slow and easy. "Progress," as an idea, was unknown. Many people believed that the world would end with the millennium, or first thousand years after Christ. But the sacred anniversary came and went without incident, and life jogged on in the green, half-empty island of fields and forests, crisscrossed with the fading tracks of ancient Rome.

††

WILLIAM: THE

SELF-MADE KING

On a steep hill in France, above the small town of Falaise in Normandy, there still stands the castle, its keep massive and square above the billowing softness of the treetops. And until 1944, certainly, the tannery still remained where it had always been, its sheds and yard grouped on the banks of the stream at the foot of the hill. But in that summer, when the Allied forces landed in Normandy to liberate Europe from Hitler, the horrors of modern warfare exploded in Falaise. Nine-tenths of the town was destroyed. Only the castle clung, eagle-proud, to its rocky perch, scarred and shaken but still itself. The core of that castle is more than nine hundred years old; the later parts are newer by a mere century or so. It is still true to say, then, that *"this* was the castle."

Here, in the year 1026, lived the young bachelor Count of Hiesmois, brother to the Duke of Normandy. To his face the Count was referred to as "Robert the Magnificent"; behind his back, he was more commonly nicknamed "Robert the Devil." And a magnificent young devil he probably was— strong-willed, passionate, swaggering, and on occasion (like all his folk) cruel. For the Dukes of Normandy, though they had been Frenchified for a century, were sprung from Viking stock. Their ancestor was that Rolf or Rollo who had brought his long ships up the Seine, and, proving too tough to be turned out, had been accepted as the duke of that region. "Northman" had become "Norman," pagan had become Christian, but some of the Viking blood still ran in their veins, though even the words on their lips had changed to French.

That was Robert, then, living in the grim square tower on the rock.

At the bottom of the hill lived Fulbert the tanner. And Fulbert had a daughter Arletta. And Arletta had attractions that Robert did not fail to notice as he rode up and down past the tannery, between his castle and the town.

A tanner's daughter was hardly suitable as a countess, but Robert fell deeply in love with her. If he could not marry Arletta, he would certainly marry no one else. Nobody could dictate to Robert the Devil.

So it was that, in the following year, 1027, a child was born to Arletta in a small dark room in the castle—little more than a windowless recess carved out of the wall of the keep that is five yards thick there. They called him William. History was to add "the Conqueror."

A few months later, Robert's elder brother died suddenly. There were those who said Robert had helped him out of the world with poison. At all events, Robert was not sorry to become Duke of Normandy in his brother's place.

William—soon to be joined by a baby sister, Adelaide—was a good-looking little boy with dark hair and gray eyes. He showed personality and strength of will from early years. People used to say, afterwards, that even as a newborn child he showed his character by the way he clutched the rushes on the floor of that dark little room where he lay. As a five-year-old he was the natural leader of his young friends, drilling and dominating them all.

The typical education of a Norman boy is summed up in what another duke had said a generation or two before. "My son must be noble among nobles, scholarly among scholars, steady in the saddle, swift in the field. He must know all the lore of the countryside, the bends of the rivers, the boundaries of meadow and woodland. He must know how to fly his falcon, cast a net, throw a javelin, slip a hound, and slay a deer." This, in general, was the course William followed, as his later life shows, except that opinions differ about his book learning. Certainly his father was in no position to lecture him on that point. He himself, when a boy, was said to have stabbed the tutor who rebuked him for idleness. After that he had taken to the forest for a time, with a band of rascally followers. He was well named Robert the Devil.

There is an old saying, "When the Devil is sick, the Devil a saint would be," and when William was seven, his father showed the truth of it. He announced he was going on a pilgrimage to the Holy Land. He was not well, and he might never return. In that case, William was to have the dukedom.

When he announced this to his assembled barons, there was a murmur of objection. William was too young. William found himself lifted in his father's brawny arms, heard his father laugh and cry: "He is only little, yes, my lords, but he will grow." Pushed to it, the barons came out with their other objection: William was basely born, his mother no rightful duchess but only a tanner's daughter. The Duke retorted that William was the only son he had or was likely to have. The barons had to give way. The dukedom was, after all, Robert's to give away as he liked. The Normans had none of that idea that the Saxons held across the Channel—the first faint gleam of democracy—that a ruler must be accepted and approved by his people.

The barons knelt and swore allegiance to the boy, and Duke Robert departed on his journey.

For a long time news of him was scarce and doubtful. A pilgrim named Pirou turned up with the report that he had met the Duke at the gates of Jerusalem. The Duke had not been well, for he was lying in a litter carried by four swarthy natives. But, with a flash of his old spirit, he had managed to joke about the situation. "You can say," he had told

Pirou, "that you met me being borne off to Paradise by four black devils!" Silence and rumors followed. At last it was confirmed that Robert had died on the way home. William was Duke of Normandy.

What did that mean? Though he had barons and bishops to act for him until he was older, William already had a fair notion of what it meant to be Duke of Normandy.

It meant that in a few years' time, when he was free of his guardians, he would be absolute lord of this little country. For, though the King of France was rather vaguely thought of as an overlord, the Norman dukes took practically no notice of him.

Normandy was a little world of its own. It lay along the coast, its pale chalk cliffs looking across the Channel to the very similar English cliffs just beyond the horizon. To the east was Flanders, to the west Brittany, with their own separate rulers, and inland, up the Seine, were the king's own territories.

A green land, Normandy, a land of woods and fields and orchards. There were towns—Rouen, Caen, Bayeux, Falaise, Harfleur—and a thick sprinkling of castles, his own and his barons'. For it was the Norman way to fight from castles or, if caught in the open, to fight on horseback with the lance. The Saxons, William learned, were quite different in their methods: they troubled less with castles and fought from choice in the open; having reached the battlefield, they preferred to dismount and fight it out with sword and ax.

Fighting was important. It was certain to play a big part in his life. William must have realized this from his earliest years. If we are to understand William—or any other nobleman of the medieval period—we must understand the reasons for this quite clearly.

Otherwise the Middle Ages will remain (as they have done to millions of puzzled school children) a meaningless muddle of sieges, rebellions, plots, raids, and family feuds. Why *did* barons fight so much? These galloping men in mail, who form so large a part of the pageant of medieval history, did not gallop solely for exercise.

When William could say to himself, "Normandy is mine now," he meant it literally. The land was his. As he could not look after it all himself, much of it was held by lesser lords or by monasteries, who paid him contributions in return. Cash played a small part in everyday life, and few coins were circulated, so the Duke's income came to him in various forms. It might be grain or eggs or fish or any other foodstuff, cloth or timber or hay, falcons or horses or hounds. Much of it would be in service —military service or labor of one sort or another.

The bigger a lord's territory, the bigger his income. Hence wars between duchies and nations.

The weaker a lord's authority, the more chance for his underlings, or vassals, to avoid paying him what they were supposed to. Hence armed rebellion and defiance when the vassal thought he could get away with it.

The larger the number of a lord's sons, the smaller the share of lands for each. Hence family feuds and civil war even between brother and brother or father and son.

True, many noblemen liked fighting for its own sake and bracketed it in their minds with hunting and other exciting sports. True, they were trained for it and, unless they became priests, no other profession was open to them. But the taste and the training did not *cause* the warfare; they developed because of the way in which the medieval world was organized.

If we are still puzzled that these knights and barons should be willing to risk death and injury, mainly to extract a larger income from their lands or to withhold due payment from their overlords, we should turn for a moment and glance at our own age. Here we see plenty of people, some perfectly honest and some less so, risking bankruptcy to make more money, and not a few dishonest ones risking prison to cheat the tax collector.

Under their mail shirts the Norman blood— under their cone-shaped helmets the Norman head —worked very much the same.

That was what the Duke of Normandy had to reckon with. And it was not easy when you were only eight or nine.

William's mother married a knight named Sir Herluin de Conteville—it was hardly safe for a woman to remain single unless she became a nun, and certainly Arletta, the despised daughter of the tanner, who had cast her spell on Duke Robert, had more than her share of enemies. She, more than most, needed the protection of a husband.

William had his guardians, appointed by his father. Anyhow, a boy of his age spent more time with the men than with any mother. But the link of family affection was strong, and when Sir Herluin and Arletta had children, William proved a stanch half brother to them. There were two boys and a girl in Arletta's second family. The elder boy, Odo, was later Bishop of Bayeux and William's lifelong helper. The younger boy was christened Robert, which was a trifle tactless on Arletta's part.

When not touring his duchy, William kept his court in Rouen, the cathedral city near the mouth of the Seine. Here, until he was entering his teens, he had the company of his elder cousin Edward, the exiled heir to the English throne, then held by Danish usurpers. This was the gentle, religious Edward who earned the nickname of "the Confessor." Growing up in Normandy, Edward picked up a preference for French ways and a healthy respect for his masterful young cousin. These facts were to be important in the future history of England and Normandy.

William was about fourteen when Edward left Rouen to become King of England, largely through the influence of the leading English earl, Godwin of Wessex. It was this Godwin's son, Harold, who was later to fight William at Hastings. So, one by one, the chief characters in the drama take the stage: Edward the Confessor, William, and Harold.

Edward married Harold's sister, Edith. There was thus a family link between them all.

William was a far-sighted person, given to long, brooding silences, and—though he could also fly into a rage—extremely patient. But even William could not possibly see, at this period, that twenty-four years after Edward's crowning, he would be a claimant to that crown himself.

It was all he could do to manage Normandy. It was a temptation to many barons to avoid paying their dues to a boy duke. There were plots and revolts. His three guardians were murdered. William called together the chief men in Normandy and on their advice took another guardian. Actually, this man, Ralph of Wacey, was one of the murderers, but there is an old principle that an ex-poacher makes the best gamekeeper, and in this case it was sound. Ralph did not betray him. But with such a guardian William had to walk warily. So, even in boyhood he learned to tread the tightrope of danger.

The worst peril came when he was twenty and had taken up his full powers as duke.

He was hunting—it was a lifelong passion of his —and there was a plot to surprise him at his lodge in the forest, at Valognes. His cousin Guy of Burgundy led the conspiracy. William was to be killed or made captive.

William had the narrowest of escapes. He rode headlong eastwards to Falaise, where he knew he could rely on the loyalty of his native town. But he could not muster enough troops of his own to deal with Guy, so he rode away to Poissy, where King Henry of France received him and promised military aid. Then followed William's famous first battle at Val-es-dunes, just east of Caen, about which Hilaire Belloc wrote a splendid (but as he said himself, "grossly unhistorical") poem:

"And now, go forward, Normandy,
  Go forward all in one.
The press was caught and trampled and it broke
From the sword and its swinger and the axe's stroke,
Pouring through the gap in a whirl of smoke
  As a blinded herd will run.
And so fled many and a very few
With mounts all spent would staggering pursue,
But the race fell scattered as the evening grew;
  The battle was over and done.

    "Like birds against the reddening day
      They dwindled one by one,
    And I heard a trumpet far away
      At the setting of the sun." *

As Belloc himself points out, it was not so much William who won the victory as the troops lent him by the King. But a great victory it was, and from that day William was able to win his own battles.

He was a man now, tall, good-looking, with high temples, a keen glance in his gray eyes, and strong,

---

* From *Sonnets and Verse,* by H. Belloc. Reprinted by kind permission of the publishers, Messrs. Duckworth.

stern features, which could sometimes soften into a smile of great charm. So far he had shown little interest in girls, but about this time he made up his mind that he would marry Matilda, the daughter of his neighbor, the Count of Flanders.

Matilda had other views. She was a beautiful girl, then about seventeen, proud of her noble ancestry (which included Alfred the Great of England), and a lover of poetry and art. She had a mind of her own. She herself had already suggested marrying an English aristocrat. He had snubbed her, and she was in the worst possible mood when her parents told her of William's proposal. Never, she retorted, would she wed the lowborn grandson of the Falaise tanner.

Her remarks (and even the most refined young ladies were apt to be outspoken in that century) were all too accurately reported to William. An insult to his parentage was something he could not bear. Once, when besieging some rebels in Alençon, he was mocked by skins hung from the battlements and the jeering cry of "Hides for the tanner!" He took a terrible revenge on the men responsible.

How, though, to deal with Matilda of Flanders? The young man did not hesitate. He took horse and galloped over the frontier to her father's palace at Lille. Before anyone could announce him, he burst into the room where she was, seized her by her long plaits, knocked her about for some moments, hurled her to the floor, and then departed as he had come, without formality.

Matilda found this passionate young man irresistible in more senses than one. She raised no further objection to the marriage. But the Church did, for there was a faint degree of relationship between the two families, and this time the authorities chose to be awkward.

William found himself up against his newest friend and adviser, a remarkable Italian monk named Lanfranc, who was destined to be one of the greatest influences in William's life. Lanfranc was more than twenty years older than he; a man of high birth and even higher intellect; a Greek scholar in an age when Greek was almost forgotten in Western Europe; a churchman, an educator, an organizer, and a lawyer. He was then prior of Bec, which he had entered because it was "the poorest monastery he could find," but which he made a renowned center of learning. When the Pope banned the proposed marriage, Lanfranc supported the Pope. William flew into another of his rages and looted the monastery lands at Bec. He banished Lanfranc from his duchy, but the prior behaved with such dignity and courage that the quarrel between them was later made up. After four years, William and Matilda ignored the ban and were married.

In the year before their wedding, William paid his first visit to England, to see his cousin King Edward, whom he had known so well in boyhood. The two countries were always in close contact, for Edward admired everything Norman and gave great offense to many of his subjects by giving high positions to men from across the Channel.

The Bishop of London was a Norman. So were some of the King's chaplains.

Normans were often surprised by the wealth and civilization of Edward's England. In size, of course, it was many times larger than their own country. It was well farmed and, as the climate was probably milder than it is now, there were vineyards in the southern districts. There were many towns and seaports and a busy traffic with the outside world. The arts and crafts reached a high standard. Matilda, later on, was to be particularly proud of a dress made for her by one of her English ladies in waiting, and even to mention it in her will. English coins were especially beautiful in Edward's reign; after the Norman Conquest they were cruder, and it was a hundred years or more before the mints regained their old quality of design. Despite Danish havoc, the monasteries were full of precious articles.

William's keen gray eyes took in the scene, and his hard head was busy. What was to happen to this country when his gentle cousin died? Edward had no son. The next heir—near in blood but far in space—lived in Hungary and was a mere name to the English. Of course, the Danes would probably try to move in and make a final effort to bring the island into the family circle of Scandinavia. Against them, the jumped-up Godwin, Earl of Wessex and Edward's father-in-law, might try to take the throne for his family.

The future was quite uncertain. No one could tell how long Edward would live. As a matter of fact, he lived nearly fourteen years after that visit of William's, whereas the powerful Godwin died quite soon afterwards. Harold, Godwin's son, took over his father's estates, and it was he who now would be the man to reckon with.

Years passed. William and Matilda had children, both boys and girls. William strengthened his control of Normandy and enlarged his power by taking over the smaller territory of Maine to the south. He won the title of "Conqueror" long before he sailed against England; for all he knew, his future might lie entirely on the Continent. He was brave, but no gambler.

He had luck that any gambler might have envied. In 1064 Harold was sailing in the Channel and was wrecked on the French coast. He was seized by the local lord, Guy of Ponthieu, with a view to ransom. William heard and wasted no time. Before Harold could be ransomed, he virtually "bought" him from Guy. It was all done under a cover of friendliness. Harold was received as an honored guest at the Norman court, but he knew that he had only exchanged one prison for another.

Men argued afterwards—and have argued ever since—just what William and Harold agreed together.

The Normans said that Harold did homage to William and became "his man," and that he promised William the crown of England when Edward died.

The English said that neither Harold nor even Edward himself could promise William any such thing, because only the Council could choose a

new sovereign. Kingship in England was an office
to which a man was elected, not a private possession
to be handed on. Anyhow, promises made under
threats were not real promises at all, and if (as some
said) William had tricked Harold into swearing—
over a hidden collection of holy relics—no such
oath was binding. As for the "homage," it depended
upon what was meant by the ceremony. Harold had
understood it simply as a formal expression of thanks
to William for saving him from Guy of Ponthieu.

Both William and Harold were largely sincere
in the views they held. The tragedy of Hastings,
two years later, was not the clash of hero and villain (from whichever side it is looked at) but the
conflict of two brave men, each having a great deal
of justification for what he did.

So Harold went back to England, where his presence was soon badly needed to deal with rebellion
in the North, with which the King could not have
coped. And within a year or so Edward fell ill during the Christmas festival and died in the first week
of the new year.

It was the fateful year of 1066.

The news crossed the sea to Normandy, and William swore one of his passionate oaths.

Harold had played him false! The dying King
had recommended Harold as his successor, the
Council had accepted his recommendation—and
Harold had accepted the crown. Not a day had
been lost. The mourners had turned from the grave
to escort Harold to his throne. The coronation had

been held in the newly built abbey of Westminster, which had been Edward's dearest project.

A lesser man than William would have raged vainly and then admitted himself beaten.

What, after all, could he do? Harold had been practical ruler of England, in Edward's name, for some time past. Now he openly wore the crown. It was the depth of winter. He had months in which to strengthen himself before any enemy could cross the sea to challenge him.

And what then? How could little Normandy challenge England? There were good English ships to meet in the Channel before even a landing could be made. Those passed, there were the swarming soldiers of England—those stalwart, dogged fellows, bigger on the average than Normans, wielding frightful Danish axes that would go through chain mail as though it were linen. And at their head would be Harold, the now-familiar figure whose abilities William had learned to respect— Harold, with his blue eyes and drooping fair mustache, Harold the brave soldier and the skillful general, under his gold-wrought standard, the Standard of the Fighting Man.

The odds seemed hopelessly balanced against success. William brooded over the problem. Were the odds as heavy as they seemed? And could the balance be altered in his favor?

The English were strong, yes. United, they could hardly be beaten. But *were* they united? Harold was not of the old royal house. He had his enemies. There were men in England who thought themselves as good as Harold. Such men would not fight for William against Harold, but they might hang back and not help, thinking that Harold and William would cancel each other out, thus leaving themselves in power.

So, thought William, England might be weaker than she seemed. Was Normandy stronger than she seemed? Or could she be made so?

Normandy could not be more united than she was. Long before, he had seen to that. Her manpower was solid behind him, but it was just not big enough to take over England. He must have more troops. Not allies—allies meant other dukes or kings in equal partnership, and he wanted no partners. Volunteers! That was the solution. Individuals and small bands, enlisting under his banner, all bound by allegiance to him . . .

William began a skillful propaganda campaign throughout Europe. It was his view of the dispute that was spread and accepted everywhere—all the more easily because it fitted in with the general practice on the Continent. Crowns *were* regarded as personal property, to be left by one king to another. William's case was that Edward had promised the crown to him and that Harold had sworn to help him. Edward's deathbed recommendation of Harold was easy to explain away. Harold's conduct was not. In Europe few people understood the English viewpoint: that neither Edward nor Harold had been free to promise anything, and that only the English could appoint an English king.

William sent the monk Lanfranc—who was now

his friend again—to Rome to see the Pope. The shrewd Italian put William's case with his usual brilliance. The Pope did not hear Harold's side at all. He decided in favor of William and blessed his enterprise, thus turning it into something like a crusade.

Volunteers began to pour in. The Pope's blessing made the expedition respectable: the promise of land and loot made it attractive. From Flanders and Brittany, from Aquitaine and Provence, even from beyond the Alps, in Italy, knights were strung along the roads leading to Normandy. They were "soldiers of fortune" in the truest sense. William smiled as the numbers mounted. With luck, everything was going to be all right.

That summer he had the devil's own luck.

He was ready to sail by mid-August, but the wind was against him and he could not set out until the end of September. That delay, however maddening it may have seemed at the time, was his salvation.

The simple problem of food and forage made it hard to keep a big army together for long. William managed it by good organization, so that his army held out in Normandy without either starving or looting the countryside. The English *fyrd,* mustered to meet William on the Sussex beaches, stayed as long as they could and then were forced to disband.

So, too, with Harold's ships patrolling the Channel. They could not keep at sea forever. They had to pass through the Dover Straits and sail around to the Thames for stores and refitting—just before the wind veered in William's favor.

Greatest luck of all, Harold Hardrada of Norway

started an invasion of his own in Yorkshire, landing early in September. It was too much for the North Country *fyrd* to deal with. King Harold had to choose between the invasion that had already started and the one that was only threatened and now looked as though it might never come. He rode northwards with his regular army and on September 25 smashed the Norwegians at the Battle of Stamford Bridge. That was the moment when the wind changed in the Channel, and three days later William launched his own attack.

If he had been able to do so a few weeks earlier, he would have met a fleet to dispute his crossing. And on the beaches he would have met the mass array of the *fyrd* from all the southern counties, Harold himself, and all the regular troops, under the golden standard of the Fighting Man. Or if the wind had stayed contrary for just a few more days, Harold would have been back from Yorkshire with at least his regulars, and time to call out the rest of his men. But it was not so. William sailed at dusk on September 28, not knowing until some time later the full total of his luck.

William led the fleet out from St. Valéry in his flagship *Mora*. Her name was appropriate, being the Latin for "delay." Her masthead lantern guided the ships behind. Her figurehead was a golden boy, whose carved eyes gazed serenely across the darkling waters toward the invisible island.

How many ships spread their wings in the wake of the *Mora?* Some say there were three thousand—

that William's half brother Odo himself contributed a hundred—but this total sounds too large, even making full allowance for all the horses and equipment. The Norman army that fought at Hastings two weeks later numbered about nine thousand men. At all events, for those days it was a great host—yet to William's dismay, when dawn came, he saw not another craft in view.

It was a hazy autumn morning. The shingly beach of Pevensey was near. William gave orders to anchor and sent a ship's boy scrambling to the masthead. At first the boy could see nothing, then he called down to say that the mist was lifting and that a whole forest of masts could be seen. The *Mora* weighed anchor and ran forward into the land-locked harbor that is now the dry land of Pevensey Levels. Exultantly, William leaped ashore—only to stumble forward on hands and knees. Quick-witted, so that superstitious men should not be dismayed, he righted himself and held up his hands, clutching sand and shingle, turning the accident into a symbolic gesture of possession.

"By the splendor of God," he roared, "I have taken *seizin* of England!" "Seizin" was the legal term meaning "possession of freehold land."

By late afternoon the ships were beached, the army ashore, and the horses at grass. It would have been very different if Harold had been there. . . .

But Harold was two hundred miles away in Yorkshire. When the news reached him, he started south. Those men who could keep up with him did so. It was a business for mounted men, and well-mounted

men, at that. Possibly some foot soldiers managed
that prodigious march by hanging on to the stirrup
leathers of the horsemen. At any rate, Harold
reached London within a week, gathered what fresh
forces he could there, and hurtled on to meet the
invaders. The last seventy miles were covered in
three days. He reached Hastings with about the
same number of men as William's, and further reinforcements trickled in, hour by hour. But whereas
the Normans were fresh, and all fighting men of
good quality, the English ranged from the pick of
the royal guard to the poorly armed local levies.
And the better part of Harold's forces were not only
tired by their almost incredible march down the
length of England, but before that they had been
cruelly mauled by the Norwegians. Stamford Bridge,
though a victory over those invaders, had not been
an easy one.

The Battle of Hastings raged throughout a whole
October day. It was touch and go all the while. William knew he could lose. That was why he had never
moved more than a mile or two from the escape
route offered by his ships.

There is no need to retell the familiar tale of that
day, but two common statements need correcting.
It is probably *not* true that the Normans led the
English to break ranks by pretending to run away:
most likely the Norman flight was genuine for the
time being, but they recovered themselves and took
advantage of the English mistake in following them.
No one was trained for so difficult and well-disci-
plined a maneuver as a pretended retreat plus re-

covery. Nor is it likely that William had a cunning idea and ordered his archers to shoot in the air with any special intention: the feeble little bows of the eleventh century (so very different from the six-foot weapon of Robin Hood) had to be pointed in the air anyhow, if their arrows were to fly any distance. In this case the English held the crest of a steep ridge, so William may have told his men to shoot even more steeply skywards. Certainly he could not have foreseen that one of the arrows—trivial, dartlike missiles compared with the cloth-yard shafts of Robin— would strike Harold full in the eye, and rob the English of their leader.

William's luck had stayed with him to the end.

His flagship had been named "delay." And "delay" was still his watchword.

Though the flower of the English army had died round their fallen king, there were thousands of fighting men who had never reached Hastings. An Alfred could have rallied them and still thrown the Normans back into the sea. And if Harold had been a member of the ancient royal family, with a son or a brother to succeed him, England could have united and defeated William. But as things were, could the English find any new leader and agree upon him?

William could not be sure. He dared not march straight on London and risk defeat. London was already so large that no army could surround it. That was to be true throughout English history:

armies might grow, as the supply problem became easier, but London always grew faster.

He took his time that autumn. He marched westwards in a wide, curving sweep, like a wolf prowling round the fold. He reached the Thames at Wallingford, far upstream. He devastated the countryside as he went, striking fear into the people. Given time to work on the fainter hearts, that fear would weaken his enemies' resistance. He crossed the Thames and swung around toward London again, cutting the roads to the north. The northern earls brought no help to the Londoners; they were playing for their own interests. So, at last, a delegation of bishops and nobles came to William and offered him the crown. On Christmas Day he was solemnly crowned King of England in Westminster Abbey.

But there was still hard fighting to come, for it took three or four years for William to master the country. There was a campaign in the West Country, where Harold's mother, Gytha, roused Devon and Dorset to resist him. There was revolt in the North, and a landing of Danes to aid the English rebels. There was a killing winter march through the Pennines to smash the resistance of Chester. There was a last famous flickering of independence by Hereward in the Fens. But William defeated all his enemies, because they never joined together.

He was clever in keeping them disunited. True, he had to keep his promises to his followers and give them English lands. True, he was privately determined to put Normans into as many key positions as he could. But he was careful never to behave like a foreign conqueror, with an open policy of favoring the outsider against the native.

He always insisted that he was King of England not by conquest but by law. He had a sincere passion for law—though often he paid more attention to the letter of it than the spirit. No Englishman was to be put out of his lands simply because he was English. If he lost his estates, it was because he had rebelled against his lawful king. French or English were to be treated exactly alike in the eyes of the law, and it was English law. It just happened that most rebels tended to be Englishmen. . . .

In the same way, though William was eager to reform the easygoing English Church, he did not turn out the English bishops and put foreigners in their places. It just happened that, as the English bishops died, the right men to replace them proved to be foreigners. By the end of his reign, there was not a single English bishop.

All this was a gradual process. There was no sudden edict, hurting everyone at once and driving people to unite and resist him. Each individual hoped that he, personally, might be lucky. It was encouraging that William paid such close heed to English law and custom, that he tried to learn English himself (he was too busy to get far with it), and that he saw to it that his youngest son Henry was taught the language.

Henry (afterwards Henry I) was English-born. Matilda had followed William as soon as it was safe enough. She had been made queen and was the first

English king's wife to add *Regina* to her signature. Saxon kings' wives had not used the title. Henry was born at Selby, in Yorkshire, two years after Hastings. By then, Robert, the eldest boy, was fourteen and William Rufus, the red-haired, was twelve. Altogether they had three sisters, named Constance, Adela, and Agatha. A big family, but not, as it turned out, a happy one. William's sons grew up to plague him and almost break his heart.

He was better at taming England. Year by year the loose, free-and-easy kingdom became more firmly organized. No great barons were defying him from petty kingdoms of their own: except on the Welsh and Scottish borders, where big forces were needed to keep out raiders, he arranged that his lords should hold estates scattered in different regions. All landowners, too, had to swear allegiance to him personally, as the king. They could not excuse disloyalty to him by saying that they had been obeying some intermediate overlord.

Twenty years after his accession, William carried his work of organization a stage further. He had the idea of a systematic survey of the whole country's wealth and resources, village by village, down to the last acre. He announced this plan when he was spending Christmas at Gloucester Abbey—he followed the old tradition of the English kings and "wore his crown," in state, three times every year for the main Christian festivals. It was always Christmas at Gloucester, Easter at Winchester, and Whitsuntide at Westminster. His plan for the survey was put into effect and became the Domesday Book, the most complete record of its kind in medieval Europe and, for that reason, the envy of all foreign historians.

William changed the face of England in several ways.

When he came, there were only three castles in the whole country. He and his barons dotted the land with castles in the Continental style. In every shire the peasants toiled to dig out moats and heap up huge mounds, which were topped at first with wooden towers and later with the stone keeps we associate with a Norman castle. William himself was responsible for the White Tower, in London, and the first castles at Windsor, Rochester, Nottingham, and a host of other key points. Countless others were built by his barons.

New churches, too, began to rise, replacing older and smaller ones. Lanfranc was made Archbishop of Canterbury at the first opportunity, and within four years of the Battle of Hastings, he had begun the rebuilding of the cathedral. Gundulf, a monk, was brought over from Bec in Normandy and made Bishop of Rochester. He not only rebuilt his cathedral but also planned the keep of Dover Castle nearby. All of the best architects were monks: William brought them over from France and even Italy. The distinctive features of Norman architecture began to spread everywhere—the round arch supported by short, massive columns, plain at base and capital; and the simple plastered walls. No stained glass relieved the severity of these churches; that did not reach England for another century.

In another, grimmer, fashion William left his mark on the scene. He enlarged the hunting grounds in Hampshire, turning out the peasants where necessary. He created the New Forest, little guessing that in years to come his son Rufus was to die there, victim of a mysterious arrow. Far worse in its consequences was his deliberate action in laying waste a vast tract of northern England, the "harrying of the North," as it was called. Its object was to weaken Northumberland so that it should not rebel against him a second time: its result was to leave that district so weak and poor that it scarcely recovered itself until the modern age of coal and iron.

William was a strange blend of mercy and cruelty. It is not fair to judge him by twentieth-century standards.

He sentenced many men to be maimed—blinded or deprived of a limb—but it was a common punishment in those days and was considered more merciful than the death penalty. It was William's pride that, apart from those killed in battle, he was responsible for hardly any man's death. He made great efforts, too, to stop the slave trade between Ireland and the ports of western England, for the Irish raiders were still active—it was they who, seven centuries before, had kidnapped St. Patrick from his home in Wales and carried him off to slavery.

He was certainly a much milder ruler than his half brother Odo, but unfortunately for the English, Odo was far too often left in charge as regent. For William divided his time fairly equally between England and Normandy. Matilda, after that first year or two, lived almost entirely in Normandy. It was in these later years that she and her ladies are said to have embroidered the Bayeux tapestry, telling the story of the Conquest in what we should now call "strip" form. The tapestry is of linen, two hundred and twenty feet long by twenty inches wide, the figures worked in woolen threads in eight different colors. As the work was done with needles, it is not strictly a tapestry at all. In a true tapestry the picture is worked into the fabric with a spindle, forming stitches across the warp.

William's last years were dark. The splendid adventure of the Conquest had been successful, he had won over the majority of his new subjects, he had found an outlet for his tremendous energies and organizing powers—but there was a strange emptiness in victory.

His sons were a disappointment, Robert especially, whom he planned to make Duke of Normandy but not King of England. They quarreled and fought, Matilda showed too much sympathy for her son, and husband and wife had their first serious difference since the far-off day of their tempestuous courtship. Then Matilda died and was buried magnificently in the abbey at Caen. William was alone.

He was an elderly man now, by the standards of that century, though still on the right side of sixty. The dark hair had thinned to baldness, the once athletic figure had thickened and coarsened into fat. But he rode on, wearily and without zest, and fought more battles against his unruly subjects in Maine or border raiders from the French king's territory.

It was these raiders that took him to Mantes, a town near the edge of Normandy. It was August, 1087. He had taken a harsh revenge upon the raiders; the town was a smouldering ruin. He had always believed in firm measures . . . just punishments . . .

Suddenly his tired charger stumbled. He was thrown sharply against the pommel of his saddle and suffered an internal injury. He could not remount, so they carried him out of the town to the abbey of St. Gervais. There he lingered for several weeks, and died on September 9. The doctors who had failed to save him fled in panic, the nobles (fearing rebellions and civil war) rode off to prepare themselves for any emergency, and the servants took the opportunity to loot the building. Even the dead man's robes and bed linen were taken. William lay deserted and almost naked on the floor.

Of the Conqueror, as of all men, the words of the burial service rang true: "We brought nothing into this world, and it is certain we can carry nothing out."

THE YEARS BETWEEN

1087-1157

Only a man's lifetime, the Bible's threescore years and ten, lies between the death of William the Conqueror and the birth of his great-great-grandson, Richard I. But in that short space there had been many changes. The strong fingers of the Normans had molded England to a new shape. Able and energetic kings (none more so than Richard's own father, Henry II) had brought more efficient government. As individuals, they wielded more power than their Saxon predecessors; Parliament and Magna Charta had yet to come. Gone was the old, easygoing Saxon spirit, in Church as well as in State. Bishops and abbots of the stern Norman pattern vied with the king's officers and the barons to ensure that the rank and file did their duty as they should. Both the medieval Church and the feudal system had reached the highest level of their organization.

There were other changes to the outward eye.

79

True, the pattern of the fields, the peasants' hovels, the spreading miles of forest were unaltered. But the age of castle building started by the Conqueror had continued, and now every county had a newish-looking stone fortress or two, crowning the more conspicuous hillocks. Most of the little Saxon churches and cathedrals had been scornfully demolished and rebuilt more magnificently, often in part with stone shipped from Normandy. Monasteries had expanded and multiplied; monks and nuns were active as farmers, teachers, nurses, and in many other ways. And as crafts and trades developed, the towns were beginning to grow.

†††

RICHARD:

THE CRUSADER

Richard—destined to be known to later ages as *Coeur de Lion* or "Lionheart"—was born at Oxford on September 8, 1157.

Oxford was then a small town. It had never fully recovered from a disastrous fire that had occurred about a century before—Domesday Book registers half the houses as in ruins—and although scholars had begun to gather there, it was to be another hundred years before the first college was founded. There was a traditional curse on any King of England entering the city, and that is no doubt why Richard's parents had their palace at Beaumont.

No trace of that palace remains except for the name Beaumont Street, now a busy thoroughfare, with theater and museum, close to the heart of the city. But when Richard saw the light of day, Beaumont Palace was well outside the Oxford boundary, perhaps a bowshot from where, very soon, the northern wall of the town was to be built.

Richard was the remarkable son of equally remarkable parents.

His father, Henry II, was one of the strongest of the medieval English kings, as he needed to be to restore order after the long civil war between his mother Queen Maud and his uncle King Stephen.

He was a powerfully built man, with a big freckled face and short reddish hair. His energy was as terrifying as his hot temper. He could outwalk and outride his courtiers, and frequently exhausted them. "He never sits down," lamented one of them. "He is always on his feet from morning till night." Even his meals were often taken standing, and court etiquette therefore prevented everyone else from sitting. Even in church he was so restless that he whispered frequently to his neighbors, or doodled. His voice, always harsh and cracked, became almost hysterical when passion seized him. The most momentous of these outbursts was the one that caused four of his knights to rush off and murder his onetime friend and then obstinate opponent, the archbishop Thomas-à-Becket at Canterbury. Altogether, an alarming parent even for a Lionheart to possess.

Richard's mother, Queen Eleanor, was herself formidable. Long years later, at the age of eighty-four, she stood a siege on behalf of her youngest son, King John. One cannot help wondering how she got on with her mother-in-law, the even more formidable Queen-Empress Maud.*

Eleanor had been Queen of France before, and

* For her story, see *The Seven Queens of England.*

if she told Richard only a tenth of her experiences (she certainly could not have told him all), he must have had an entertaining childhood. She was a gay, frivolous society woman, as fantastic in her dress as King Henry was simple in his. But she must have assured Richard she was not empty-headed and she cared deeply for the things of the spirit. Why, in her younger days at the French court, she had not only heard the renowned Bernard preach the second Crusade but she had been so moved by his eloquence that she had "taken the Cross" herself and volunteered for the expedition!

Sitting at her feet, the future adversary of Saladin listened (we can only guess with what private thoughts) to his mother's carefully edited account of her own adventures in the Holy Land. How she and her ladies had put on armor and drilled in public. How they had scornfully sent their distaffs to those knights of their acquaintance who had not yet volunteered to fight the Saracens. How they had set off for Palestine with an immense armament, not forgetting tents of gold-embroidered silk, cushions, and a fashionable wardrobe for off-duty moments. What interesting places they had seen, and what delightful (or impossible) people they had met during the long journey across Europe.

And what about the fighting, any boy must have asked with some impatience, and certainly a boy of Richard's type?

Well. . . . At this point we may imagine that his mother became a trifle evasive. The Crusaders had, in fact, been soundly beaten by the Saracens. Eleanor and her ladies had made a dramatic escape; her then husband, King Louis, had saved himself by climbing a tree; but the silken tents and cushions had been abandoned, along with most of their clothes and all hope of delivering Jerusalem from the infidel.

And what happened then? Eleanor may well have smiled at her memories. She had gone to Antioch, where the handsome young Raymond of Poitou was king. He was actually her uncle, but that had not prevented her flirting with him. There had been other admirers, too. Eleanor, with her hot southern blood, could never resist the temptations of a love affair.

She was a married woman, of course. But—was she? She had begun to wonder. If you pored long enough over the family trees of European royalty, you found that she and King Louis were fourth cousins. Strictly speaking, they should never have married. Strictly speaking, they were *not* married. Modern divorce was unknown in the Middle Ages, but the rich and powerful had nearly always another device in reserve, the excuse of a forgotten family relationship.

Back in Paris, Eleanor's doubts had grown stronger from the moment when she met Geoffrey the Handsome, the young husband of the Empress Maud. She had fallen madly in love with him, but he had died. When his son Henry came to Paris, she fell in love with him instead. Her marriage with King Louis was dissolved, and that, Eleanor may have concluded, "was how I married your dear father."

They had certainly not lived happily ever after.

It would have been strange if they had, two such difficult and different characters. King Henry was fifteen years younger than his queen, and later, at Woodstock not far from Oxford, he was to have his own unlawful connection with the Fair Rosamund de Clifford. A legend was to grow up that he had kept Rosamund hidden in a maze, and that Eleanor found her way in by using a thread, as in the Greek legend, and poisoned her rival. The fact is that Eleanor, by then, had so fallen out with Henry that she was kept under arrest and let out only when it was absolutely essential that she should appear in public as Queen beside her husband.

These events were still in the future when Richard was small. He had a brother, Henry, two years older, and another, Geoffrey, a year younger than himself. When he was ten, another boy was born, also at Beaumont Palace, that John who was one day to grant the Magna Charta. And there were three sisters in all: Maud, Eleanor, and Joan.

Richard was his mother's favorite. None of the boys liked their father, though John, being much the youngest, did not come out in open rebellion. Richard had a special link with his mother, for it was planned that he should eventually inherit the rich French Duchy of Aquitaine, which was her own family possession. Aquitaine comprised the southern third of France, including the romantic region of the troubadours.

Perhaps it was from his mother that Richard first learned to love music and poetry. We know that later his friends included such famous minstrels as

Blondel de Nesle and Bertrand de Born, and that
he composed songs both in French and in Provençal.
In his private chapel, far from whispering or doo-
dling as his father had done, he used to walk up and
down conducting the choir.

Richard's childhood was full of color and movement. His mother brought the brilliance of southern
France to the English court, and that court was
itself continually traveling from castle to castle or
crossing the narrow seas to the Continent, for, what
with her own vast Duchy of Aquitaine and King
Henry's territories in Normandy, Maine, and Anjou, the English royal family controlled the greater
part of what is France today.

Richard's early memories were therefore divided
between the two countries. There was a gay Christmas at Marlborough Castle when he was seven: the
last time he saw his mother rule the revels of a
really happy English family Christmas. After that,
the clouds began to gather around his parents' marriage. The next May, his mother took him and his
elder sister to Normandy to join his father, who had
gone before them. The King was by then in the
midst of his fateful quarrel with Becket, and even
a seven-year-old boy could feel that the atmosphere
was heavier than usual.

There were, of course, returns to England—returns to the very palace where he was born, and
where, ten years later, brother John was born. Richard had always a strong affection for this younger
brother: even when John was treacherous to him,

Richard would always forgive him. It was natural to feel protective toward him as the baby of the family, the late, last son whom his father somewhat cruelly nicknamed "Lackland" because there was no inheritance left to promise him. John's reddish curly head never came much above Richard's shoulder—as men they were five-foot-six and six-foot-two respectively—but what John lacked in height he made up for in sly humor and charm. Richard was amused by John and sorry for him, especially when his name was put down for admission as a monk at Fontevrault Abbey. John made it clear, as he grew older, that he was not suited to the monkish life, and no further attempt was made to force him into it.

Richard's thoughts were now less on Oxford and England than on the sunny realm of Aquitaine. That was where it was planned his future would be. When he was eleven, he went with his father and elder brother to meet the King of France at Montmirail. There was an impressive ceremonial of "doing homage," for in theory even King Henry acknowledged a kind of French overlordship so far as his Continental lands were concerned. When he had thus paid homage, Richard's elder brother Henry knelt and paid homage for Brittany, Anjou, and Maine. Finally it was Richard's turn, for the Duchy of Aquitaine.

When this was completed, Richard was solemnly betrothed to the French princess Aloysia, King Louis' daughter by a second marriage. As the young couple were still only children, there was no question of a wedding for some years.

More to Richard's taste was the ceremony, just before his fifteenth birthday, when he was installed as duke in the abbey church of St. Hilary at Poitiers. He was enthroned in the abbot's chair, and the sacred lance and banner of the dukedom were placed in his hands by the Archbishop of Bordeaux and the Bishop of Poitiers. Later he went on to Limoges, where a great procession came to meet him. The holy ring of St. Valeria the Martyr was put upon his finger, and all the people shouted, acclaiming him as their new duke.

Richard had come into his heritage, it seemed. But it was an uneasy one. Duke he might be, but he was still under the guardianship of his mother—and by now the split between his parents was open. Eleanor was plotting against King Henry, and she persuaded her three elder sons to side with her. First young Henry fled from his father's side in Normandy and went to King Louis. Then Richard and his younger brother Geoffrey went from Aquitaine to join them. John was still too much of a child to be involved.

In Paris they swore a solemn oath. They would not desert the French king or make any separate peace with their father. King Louis, in turn, would help the young Henry to the throne of England.

It is very hard for the modern mind to understand these medieval family feuds. The first thing to realize is that the fathers and sons in conflict were not trying to kill one another. Thus, on a later occasion when Richard's forces were chasing his father's out of a blazing town, Richard galloped forward without any

arms and at great risk to his life, simply to make sure
that no personal hurt was done to his father.

The mentality of the people quarreling can be
imagined best in terms of a gigantic family row, mag-
nified by the size of the inheritances involved, by the
strong passions of the various individuals, which they
were not accustomed to control, and by the fact that
each was backed by a band of supporters and sympa-
thizers. To these men war was a sport. A campaign,
with a few skirmishes, was scarcely more dangerous
than a hard season of modern polo. If taken prisoner,
you were politely treated and then ransomed: so,
even to the enemy, you were more useful alive than
dead. War was hardest on the lower classes: their
houses and fields suffered, and if they were among the
fighting men, they were more likely to be killed,
since they were not worth ransoming. Their point of
view was not always forgotten, but it was seldom
allowed to spoil the game for their rulers.

At sixteen, Richard was knighted by King Louis
and was henceforth fully qualified to share in the
sport of chivalry. He still did not marry Aloysia. Indeed, the engagement dragged on for years, but it
was a political one, and in the end, for political reasons, never came to anything.

The details of the civil wars and rebellions, sometimes between Henry II and his sons, sometimes between Richard and his brothers, sometimes between
Richard and his various French opponents, matter
no more than the scores of last year's football
matches. But Richard could claim, as a man, that he

had learned his soldiering in the field and that his skill in arms was acquired in battle, not in mock fights and tournaments. He was only twenty-one when he established himself as a general of the first rank by capturing the fortress of Taillebourg, which had never been taken before and which had been considered impregnable. Richard took it after a ten-day siege and razed it to the ground.

By that time his mother had lost her leading position in the family feud. In the first year of the revolt against King Henry she had been captured while trying to reach the French king's territory in disguise—some said, wrapped in a nun's habit, others, that she was dressed as a man and riding astride. At any rate, from that time onwards, the King kept her under control.

When Richard was twenty-five, his elder brother died, and this made him heir to the English crown. His father suggested that he should hand over some of his Aquitaine inheritance to John, and, when Richard refused, encouraged John to make war against his brother. But Richard was always able to deal with John, and ready to forgive him afterwards.

Just at this time Richard met Berengaria, daughter of King Sancho of Navarre, the little Spanish kingdom at the western end of the Pyrenees. He was attracted to her, but he was still supposed to be engaged to the French princess.

Two years later, his younger brother Geoffrey died. King Henry's unmanageable sons were now reduced to two—and of these John kept up a show of obedience to his father until almost the end.

Late the next year, tremendous news burst over Christendom, which altered the whole of Richard's life.

Since the First Crusade of 1096-1099, Jerusalem had been the capital of a Christian kingdom, and the holy places and relics had been safe for pilgrims to visit. Now a new Saracen leader, Saladin, had arisen. He had defeated the Christians, captured their king, Guy of Lusignan, and seized the Cross itself, the most sacred relic of all. It had been sent to Baghdad and buried under the threshold of the city gate, so that every passer-by should tread it underfoot.

The news reached Richard one November evening at Tours. He was a religious man and a fighter. He needed no emotional sermon to stir his blood. First thing the next morning, he went to an archbishop and vowed to go on another Crusade, to rescue the Holy City and, God willing, the Cross as well.

Such ventures could not be planned in a moment. The very news, sensational though it was, had taken several months to reach France. Now it was necessary to collect money, men, and ships. The scheme was nothing less than a sea-borne invasion on a grand scale at the far side of the then known world. Richard was still preparing for it, more than eighteen months later, when another piece of important news reached him; this also, by a coincidence, at Tours.

His father was dead; he therefore was King Richard the First of England.

His first act was to hurry to his father's funeral at

Fontevraud. His next, to send word to England, ordering the release of his mother and appointing her to govern until he could. Only after three weeks did he cross the Channel. His mother met him at Winchester, with all the chief bishops and barons. He was given a warm welcome, not least from the common people.

All people under arrest for offenses against the Forest Law were released. All men outlawed for the same reason could return to their homes without fear. Many other offenders were set free and pardoned. After the efficient justice of Henry II, a milder breeze of forgiveness was blowing across the land. John shared in it. Richard was ready to let bygones be bygones.

He was not forgetting his Crusader's vow. If he devoted himself for the moment to his new kingdom, it was because he knew that, as king, he would be better able to fit out an expedition.

On the other hand, in pushing forward with his plan, he did not feel that he was neglecting England. His father had organized the government so well that for the first time in history it could be trusted to run smoothly when the king's back was turned. Richard personally knew little of this country that until recently he had never expected to rule.

Above all, Richard was vowed to the Crusade, and he was a man of his word. Not for nothing had his troubadour friend Bertrand de Born nicknamed him *Richard Oc-e-No,* "Richard Yea-and-Nay," meaning that his "yes" was yes, and his "no" was no. Richard seldom swore oaths in daily matters, as other men did. A simple statement or promise was enough.

The Crusades meant very different things to different people. They had meant fashionable excitement to his mother. To many—landless knights and cutthroat adventurers—they meant the chance of loot, perhaps even the carving out of new estates and kingdoms in captured territory. Such men cared little whether they robbed the Saracens or their fellow Christians in Eastern Europe. To shipowners, to contractors and businessmen of all kinds, a Crusade was a golden opportunity to make quick profits.

Richard was perhaps one of the few who undertook the venture without selfish motives.

But first, on September 3, 1189, just before his thirty-second birthday, there was another solemn oath that even Richard Yea-and-Nay took willingly— the threefold coronation oath: to maintain the peace of the Church, to suppress injustice, and to promote equity and mercy.

This coronation, in Westminster Abbey, is a landmark in the history of the ceremony, for it has been used as a model at all succeeding coronations.

Richard made a knightly figure as he stood before the altar and was solemnly arrayed in the robes of his great office. Few men present could remember any English king but Henry—and Henry, though powerful and athletic, had been anything but romantic with his bow legs, his cropped, thinning hair, and his florid complexion.

The new king was tall and carried his chin high. He had the long straight legs which, when repeated in his descendant, Edward I, gave that king the nickname "Longshanks." His features were fine and regular: not for nothing was he the son of the lovely Eleanor of Aquitaine and the grandson, on the other side, of Geoffrey the Handsome, of Anjou. His hair was of the reddish-gold that was common in the Plantagenet family, and he wore a close-trimmed beard. His complexion was fair, his eyes blue, with a sparkle that could blaze into anger when his pride or his beliefs were touched.

The coronation service was followed by three days of solemn festivities, carried out with more decorum than usual. No ladies were allowed at the banquets, and the clergy were given the seats of honor. Jews also were barred from the proceedings. There were, of course, no Jews among the nobility. Being unable to take a Christian oath, they were unable to hold land: and as Christians were not supposed to lend money at interest (and were naturally unwilling to lend it for nothing), the Jews had been more or less driven to banking as an occupation. Richard was not himself anti-Jewish, but he felt that his coronation was, first and foremost, a Christian rite.

Unfortunately, some Jews went to the palace doors on the first evening, bearing gifts for him. They were set upon by the ignorant mob and driven away. Richard, hearing the noise outside, sent some of his officers to see what was the matter, but they were too late to do anything. A savage anti-Jewish riot had begun and swept through London. Jews were murdered and their houses looted. As in Eastern cities in our own century, there were always plenty of people ready to turn a political or a religious riot into an opening for theft or personal revenge.

Richard was grieved that his coronation should have been marred in this way. It was impossible to find and punish the guilty, but he at once sent orders to every part of England that the Jews should be left in peace. So long as he remained in the country there was no more persecution.

As a King of England Richard has almost no historical importance: of his ten years' reign, he spent less than ten months in his kingdom. In one thing only he affected its future, and that was by accident.

As the medieval towns grew in size, they all had one ambition—to win their freedom from the local landowner (it might be a baron or a monastery) who had ruled local affairs when they were mere villages. Such a landowner could levy tolls on their markets, and in one way or another skim the cream off their increasing prosperity. So what every town wanted was a charter from the king, giving it the right to control its own affairs. All through the Middle Ages we see this struggle between the middle-class townsmen and the landed nobility or the Church authorities.

Richard was not interested in the development of local government, but he was interested in money for the Crusade. He was prepared to seal any number of charters if the towns would buy them from him. "I would sell London," he cried, "if I could find a buyer." It was just because he was more interested in the Crusade than in his kingdom that, without realizing it, he cleared the way for the English towns to move forward.

Some say that Richard was equally ready to sell public offices, and even bishoprics, to the highest bidder, but this is not entirely true. He did gather donations from men he appointed, but he did not always choose the man who offered most if that man was not also the most suitable.

Just before Christmas he left for Normandy. The Crusade was to start in the spring. He was to be joined in it by the King of France, now Philip Augustus. Bishop William of Ely was to govern England in his absence, with the rank of Chief Justiciar. Brother John, though provided for with ample lands and income, was not to interfere.

For months Richard had been busy enrolling men and commandeering ships and horses. The English vessels were to make the long voyage from their home ports to Marseilles, via Gibraltar. Here Richard would embark with the army he had brought overland through France from his assembly point at Tours. The crossing of the Mediterranean to the port of Acre, in Syria, could be made in fifteen days.

Tours, the old town by the Loire, was humming with activity. Knights and men-at-arms, crossbowmen and siege engineers, armorers and farriers, grooms and camp followers of every kind poured in to enroll under the banner of the Lionheart. Here, in the same town where he had taken the Cross, and from the same archbishop's hands, Richard received the symbolic staff of a pilgrim. He leaned on it, testing it, and it broke under his weight. Those who believed in omens wondered if that boded ill luck for the whole venture.

Philip Augustus and his army joined Richard for the march down the Rhone valley. Then, to ease the problems of food and transport and billets, they divided again. Philip preferred a shorter sea trip, within safe reach of the Italian coast, so he made for Genoa. His main body, lacking ships, went by land down the length of Italy. The two kings were to meet again and concentrate their forces at Messina in Sicily.

Richard's ships were late. After a week he refused to stay at Marseilles any longer. So, as the old record says (quaintly sounding to modern ears), he "hired two large busses and twenty well-armed galleys" and set off. In the twelfth century a "buss" was a transport ship carrying one large square sail.

Any idea of a fifteen-day passage to Syria had by now been abandoned. Exact time schedules were impossible. There were a hundred and one factors to cause delay. Sincere though Richard was in his desire to reach the Holy Land, it was, in fact, not fifteen days but ten months that passed from the day he set out from Marseilles until the day he landed in Syria.

He took his time, coasting down the west of Italy, knowing that his fleet had still to overtake him at Messina. Growing tired of the slow-moving, uncomfortable ships, he went ashore and did a good deal of sight-seeing around Naples, though he refused the Pope's invitation to visit Rome. Riding down through Calabria, he became involved in a village brawl, through trying to seize a falcon that had taken his fancy. The peasants went for him with sticks and stones, and Richard threw stones back at them. The trouble was probably due to language difficulty, for Richard was openhanded and probably meant to offer a generous price for the bird. He deliberately refrained from using more than the flat of his sword, and, finding that he could not beat off his attackers without badly hurting them, he was not too proud to run away.

He spent more than six months in Sicily. There were all kinds of matters to be settled. His sister Joan was there: she had been married to the King of Sicily, who had recently died, and there was her future to be arranged. There were questions to be discussed with the French king: was Richard, or was he not, going to marry Princess Aloysia? The answer to this question was brought by Queen Eleanor, who, despite her great age, arrived in Italy with Princess Berengaria. Richard announced that he would marry Berengaria, and the engagement to Aloysia was finally broken. Queen Eleanor started back briskly, after staying a mere four days, and the Spanish princess remained behind with Richard's sister as chaperone.

These and other matters occupied the winter. The delay was unavoidable, anyhow. Sea captains did not sail during the winter if they could help it: neither the ships nor the seamanship of those days was good enough. With great fleets and convoys it would have been suicide to face the open sea in the bad season; and when Richard did at last put forth from the harbor of Messina, on April 10, it was with a positive armada.

First went three great busses, or "dromonds" as they were called in the Mediterranean. In one of these sailed Queen Joan, leaving her late husband's kingdom, and with her went Berengaria, sometimes known as "the Damsel of Navarre."

Behind them, line after line, and each line longer than the one in front, glided the rest of the fleet— first thirteen ships, then fourteen, twenty, thirty, forty, seventy—a mighty arrowhead aimed at the coast of Syria. The last line consisted of war galleys, the rest were dromonds or smaller transport vessels called "ushers," tublike craft without oars. A dromond carried forty knights and their war horses, forty foot soldiers, and a crew of fifteen sailors, together with arms and armor, a whole year's food and forage, and a portion of Richard's treasure. For fear of shipwreck, he had divided it among the fleet. An usher held about half as much as a dromond. One of the biggest items in the loading plan was the spare horse taken for every knight in the army. Richard knew that spare horses were essential in such a hot climate, when riders were so heavily armored. All these horses, and their fodder, had to be fitted in somewhere.

As soon as the armada had cleared the Strait of Messina, Richard and his war galleys put on speed and moved up to the head of the convoy. Richard was at home aboard ship. Though his experience of the sea had gone little further than the occasional Channel crossing, he showed himself an efficient commodore. "As a hen leads her chickens out to feed," wrote one chronicler, "he led his mighty fleet." Each vessel kept within hailing distance of its neighbors, each line was within trumpet signal of those in front and behind it. The escort galleys adjusted their speed to that of the slower craft, and the flagship, with a bright lantern shining after dark, set the course for all. Richard was not seasick, like many of his followers, and the worst weather did not affect his high spirits.

And certainly there was bad weather. A tiresome calm gave place to contrary winds and then to a storm. The ships tossed and rolled, the oarsmen fighting to control their long oars, the horses stamping and whinnying in terror. The neat lines of vessels sagged and buckled. When daylight returned, Richard found he had lost touch with twenty-five of them, including the dromond which held Berengaria and his sister. He steered for the island of Rhodes, just off the mainland of Asia, but though he waited hopefully there for three days, the missing ships did not arrive.

In fact, at that moment some of them were meeting fresh dangers off the south coast of another island, Cyprus. This large island was much farther east. It was the last steppingstone on the long journey to the Holy Land. It was supposed to be part of the Eastern Empire, and thus Christian, but actually its governor, Isaac Comnenus, had set himself up as an independent "emperor." He paid no heed to his

distant master in Byzantium and was more inclined
to help the Saracens than the Crusaders.

Two ships were wrecked on the rocks as they tried
to enter the harbor of Limassol. The ship containing
Queen Joan and Berengaria swung about just in
time and rode out the bad weather in the open sea.
When at last they were able to make port, they dared
not land. Isaac had seized those Crusaders who had
scrambled ashore from the wreck, and only by great
courage had they fought their way to freedom. Now,
with soft words and handsome presents, he tried to
lure the ladies ashore. At last, with many misgivings,
they told him they would land the next day.

Luckily, Richard's galley, with the rest of the fleet
dotting the sea in his wake, appeared before they
could do so. His polite inquiry brought an insulting
answer from the self-appointed emperor. Isaac mustered all his forces and drew them up behind a barri-
cade at the water's edge. Richard ordered his knights
and crossbowmen into the boats and led the landing
party himself. The air hissed and sang with arrows
and bolts. The Crusaders were at a disadvantage,
packed tightly in the little boats and unprotected
against their hidden enemies. Man after man
slumped wounded over the gunwale. The knights
were helpless, the archers had scarcely elbow room
to level their crossbows, and no clear target to aim
at. But as the water grew shallower, Richard leaped
out and waded ashore, brandishing his sword. His
men followed. The men of Cyprus deserted the bar-
ricade. Isaac galloped off on his famous bay Arab,
Fauvel. Richard seized a baggage horse, with a sack-

cloth saddle and rope stirrups, and on this makeshift charger thundered after his enemy, challenging him to "come and joust." Isaac did not even pause to acknowledge the invitation.

Richard made sure of the town and then got his horses ashore. First thing the next morning, he pushed inland with a patrol of fifty horsemen, and suddenly found himself looking down upon Isaac's camp.

One of his companions turned to him—Hugh de la Mare, a secretary who had donned arms to join the patrol. "Come away, sire," he begged, "their numbers are too overwhelming."

"Get you to your own writing business, sir clerk," the King answered. "Leave matters of chivalry to us!"

He was not going to lose the advantages of a surprise, and he knew that the main body of Crusaders was not far behind. He ordered the charge, and the little band of knights swept down the hill. Richard himself made for Isaac's standard. The emperor escaped, but his standard bearer went down, and Richard plucked the gold-embroidered flag from his hands. The rest of the Crusaders arrived before the Cypriots could rally, and there was a six-mile chase before the enemy found refuge in their native hills.

The ladies had by now landed in Limassol, and there, on May 12, in a dim little chapel of the Norman fortress, Richard and Berengaria were married. They had intended to wait until they reached the Holy Land, but the journey was proving so much longer and so much more adventurous than they had expected that it seemed better to postpone their union no longer. After the wedding, the bride was immediately crowned Queen of England. Berengaria was not only remarkable in celebrating her coronation so far from Westminster, but she was fated to be the only Queen of England who never set foot in the country.

While the festivities were still going on, Isaac asked for a peace conference. Richard rode out and met him in an orchard of fig trees close to the seashore. Richard was gloriously arrayed in a tunic of rose-colored samite, or silk. Over it was a great cloak of silver tissue covered with solid silver half-moons and blazing suns. His cap was scarlet, his spurs and sword hilt golden, his scabbard chased with silver. He rode a fine Spanish charger, to rival the emperor's Fauvel, and on his saddle were two rampant lion cubs in gold, snarling at each other.

Richard was by no means wasting time by these dealings with Isaac. Cyprus was a convenient base—almost an essential base—for the food supplies of any army invading the Holy Land. Cyprus must be made safe for the Crusade. Isaac's double dealings with the Saracens must be stopped.

The two kings duly met, and Richard stated his demands. Isaac pretended to agree and promised to serve under Richard in the Crusade, with five hundred knights. But at the first opportunity, after they had exchanged the kiss of peace, Isaac slipped out of the tent, mounted Fauvel, and fled once more. There was further fighting. A bout of fever hindered Richard, but in spite of everything it took him only fifteen days all told to complete the conquest of Cyprus.

At the end, the slippery Isaac groveled before him, begging that at least he should not be put in irons. Richard agreed with a contemptuous curl of his lip —and then ordered that fetters of solid silver should be made for him. Isaac was handed over to the Knights Hospitalers and died three years later in their fortress at Markab, near Mount Lebanon. Richard kept Fauvel for his own use. Then, with Berengaria, he embarked again. At last the way was clear to the Holy Land.

The French king had arrived six weeks before him and had taken charge of the siege of Acre, which had already been in progress for a long time. Saladin was not in the city. He lay in the hills outside, with his army of quick-moving, light-armed horsemen, harassing the Crusaders from the rear.

Richard brought new life to the siege. He was an expert both on fortification and on siege methods. He had brought giant catapults with him—he had brought even the stones for them to hurl, special flinty stones from Sicily that burst into deadly fragments as they crashed over the enemy battlements. Even when he was struck down by malaria, he had himself carried around the trenches on a stretcher, loosing an occasional bolt from his crossbow. He was a fine shot, and he never disdained any form of military service. When need arose, he would labor with his hands like the roughest pioneer.

Acre surrendered. The garrison marched out as prisoners. One of the conditions was that Saladin should hand over the Cross, which, contrary to the original report that had maddened Richard, had not been sent to Baghdad but was in safe, respectful keeping. Saladin allowed some of the Crusaders to inspect it, under flag of truce. But he did not give it up by the appointed date, nor did he confirm the rest of the agreement that his garrison had made. The Crusaders would not set free such a host of prisoners, and they could not spare men to guard them. They therefore carried out a sickening cold-blooded massacre of the Saracens. Richard, as joint leader of the Crusade, must bear a great share of the guilt. But the action did not shock the people of his own day. Not one of the chroniclers wrote a word of criticism, and even his enemy Saladin continued to admire him as the soul of chivalry. The twelfth-century eye saw the action as just.

Richard won more bitter hatred from his fellow Crusader, the Duke of Austria, who had planted his banner on one of the towers in the sector allotted to the King. Richard had it pulled down and trampled on. The Duke never forgave him, and waited for his chance of revenge. Such was the mental outlook of chivalry.

The campaign plan now fell into two parts. First, a southward march of seventy miles down the narrow strip between the hills and the sea to the port of Jaffa. Second, a right-angle turn and a thrust inland to Jerusalem.

The plan was doomed to failure. King Philip had already seen enough fighting, and was well satisfied with the capture of Acre. He sent messengers to beg

Richard to release him from his vow: the Frenchmen delivered their message with tears of shame in their eyes. Richard could not keep such a reluctant ally. He rode on with only his own forces.

After fierce fighting and terrible hardships, he battled to within sight of the city he had come to deliver. But he refused to look, from that distant hilltop, upon a place he now had to admit he could never capture, so long as Saladin was alive. A treaty of peace was made, and Richard, again racked with fever, was carried aboard his ship.

"Oh, Holy Land," he groaned as the coast grew dim in the distance, "I commend thee to God. May He of His mercy grant me life to bring thee aid. For it is my hope and resolve, by His good will, to come back."

Like Odysseus of old, Richard found his return journey quite as adventurous as the outward voyage.

Berengaria and Joan had gone ahead by another route. Romantic in other ways, the Lionheart was not an ardent lover. He had seen little of his wife during the campaign—that was understandable— and now he was content to travel separately; and, as it turned out, they by no means hastened to each other's arms when at last it was possible to meet again.

Richard's choice of a route home has puzzled many. It is supposed that, when he recovered from his most recent bout of illness, he was bored and depressed by the failure of the Crusade. He went

looking for trouble, and in that, at least, he was bril-
liantly successful.

When the facts are studied, Richard's route seems
more sensible, though he was certainly foolhardy in
some of the things he did.

He began by making for Marseilles. Then he received word that his enemies in France were plotting
to seize him when he landed, and that King Philip
himself favored the scheme. Richard's great army
was now disbanded, he was traveling with only a few
personal companions, and he was not going to step
into an obvious trap.

He could have turned toward Gibraltar and sailed
straight to England. But it was now November,
a dangerous season for the Bay of Biscay. He therefore decided to travel by the easterly land route,
through Austria and Germany. He overlooked the
little matter of the trampled banner at Acre, and he
forgot that he had an Austrian enemy as bitter as any
in France.

He changed course and sailed up the Adriatic to
Corfu. Three galleys lay off the island. Richard put
out in a small boat and hailed them. They were
pirate craft and answered him with a volley of arrows. The King then congratulated them on their
fighting spirit and suggested that they should carry
him and his staff to the port of Ragusa, now Dubrov-
nik in Yugoslavia, for a payment of two hundred
silver marks.

The bargain was not so crazy as it sounds. The
Adriatic was a perilous sea, and its rocky coasts of-

fered few places of refuge. There could be no safer pilot than a local pirate. And if there was any treachery, Richard and his knights would not have been easy passengers to overcome. Even the pirates could see that honesty was the best policy, for this one trip at least.

Richard's common sense was shown when they ran into such a violent storm that, despite all their seamanship and local knowledge, the pirates barely managed to avoid shipwreck. Richard vowed that if only they came safely to land, he would spend a hundred thousand ducats on building a church at that spot. Finally he reached shore on a rocky island just outside the port of Ragusa. After some hesitation, and with the Pope's approval for the slight alteration in his vow, Richard spent most of the money on rebuilding the cathedral in Ragusa itself. But the Benedictine monks on the island were not forgotten, and their own little church was rebuilt as well.

Voyaging on, when he had seen the work started, Richard ran into another storm. This time his ship was actually wrecked, and he struggled ashore somewhere in the Gulf of Venice. At this point he wisely decided that he was not equipped to travel in state as the King of England. He would be too tempting a prey for possible enemies. "A king's ransom" was not an empty phrase in the twelfth century; it was a golden dream that, once in a while, a bold enough villain might turn into reality.

So Richard disguised himself as "Hugh the merchant," a pilgrim returning from the Holy Land, and sent word to the Count of Gorizia nearby, asking for safe conduct. Wisely, he backed his request with a present; unwisely—forgetting that merchants did not make presents quite on the royal scale—he sent a ruby ring of considerable value.

"His name is not Hugh," said the Count as he studied the gift. "It is Richard, the King."

He promised the safe conduct, but Richard, knowing that his secret was out, took no further chances. Buying horses, he and his friends started off in the middle of the night. The Count chased after them and captured eight. Richard and the rest slipped through the Alps into Carinthia, but there was now a regular hue and cry after them.

At Freisach the local baron had a servant named Roger, a Norman who had been with him for twenty years. He sent Roger to visit all the lodging houses where pilgrims stayed, promising him a huge reward if he could find the King. It did not take Roger long to identify the speech and figure of the great Plantagenet. But neither the promised reward nor his loyalty to his master could outbalance his feeling for the man who was King of England and Duke of his own native Normandy. With tears in his eyes, he told Richard that he would never betray him. He must escape at once. Roger gave him a fresh horse and went back to his master, saying it was a false rumor that Richard was in the town.

Meanwhile, with only two companions, one a youth who could speak German, Richard slipped away. For three days and nights they pushed on as fast as their beasts could carry them. At last, exhausted and famished, they were forced to call at an inn near Vienna. They had no small change with which to pay, but only some gold bezants, coins then worth between ten and twenty shillings and, in modern money, vastly more. The youth was sent into Vienna to get change, and suspicions were aroused. On a second journey he was silly enough to carry his master's fine gloves thrust into his belt. He was arrested and tortured until he admitted that his master was indeed the English King. Richard's arch enemy, Leopold, Duke of Austria, was himself in Vienna. He sent men to surround the inn. Richard said he would surrender his sword only to the Duke in person. Leopold hurried to the spot and had the immense satisfaction of receiving it. This happened a few days before Christmas, but that year, 1192, it was a cheerless Christmas for Richard, closely guarded in the remote mountain fortress of Dürnstein, overlooking the Danube. Guards watched him day and night with drawn swords, for the Lionheart was already a legend of ferocity and they were taking no chances.

Richard was kept prisoner for just over a year, first by the Duke of Austria, later by the German Emperor Henry, who struck a bargain with the Duke. He was moved from one castle to another. Possibly to reduce the chances of a rescue attempt, or possibly because news traveled so slowly, the authorities in England were for a long time kept in ignorance of his whereabouts. There is a story, which may or may not be true, that his friend Blondel, the minstrel, wandered from castle to castle singing a song they had composed together, until an answering voice through the bars revealed that he had found the King. Certainly the official delegates sent out from England, the Abbot of Robertsbridge and the Abbot of Boxley, had to wander all over western Germany and then came upon Richard only by good luck, as he was being moved from one prison to another. And it is equally certain that Richard, in his captivity, whiled away the time with minstrelsy, for we have a song he composed in both French and Provençal versions. One verse goes:

"Do the lads know, in Anjou and Touraine,
Those lusty bachelors, those lively lords,
That these foul walls their captive king constrain?
Will they not bring me aid with loyal swords?
Alas! no faith, no courage, now remain.
Idle are sighs, and I must bear my chain."

During that year of Richard's captivity the news filtered through Christendom that his Saracen opponent, Saladin, had died of typhoid fever within a few months of the Crusaders' departure. It was a bitter thought for Richard. If only the French king had not left him, if only they had stayed a little longer . . . the Holy Land might by now have been theirs. But the only man capable of seizing it was kept like a caged beast by one who had been his comrade in the expedition.

Richard could not be rescued. He had to be ransomed, and England raised the immense sum demanded—150,000 marks—in record time. This says much for the efficient way in which his father had

organized the government of the country. It says
much, too, for Richard's popularity with the people
whom he scarcely knew. Especially as John was plotting to have his brother kept prisoner forever, and
actually offering a cash sum to the Emperor for
every month that he held Richard captive. Luckily
their mother was still watching over the interests of
her favorite son. The ancient Queen Eleanor knew
her wily John and was able to hinder his schemes.

At last Richard was released. He came back to
England and went through a second ceremony of
coronation at Winchester, as if to remove the stain
of his captivity and to proclaim that he was home in
all his glory as the King. But before this ceremony
could take place he had to deal with various barons,
supporters of John, who were in revolt against him.

Nottingham Castle was one of several great strong-
holds that refused to surrender until their defenders could be sure that Richard was really home. Envoys were sent out under a flag of truce. "What do
you think?" he demanded. *"Am* I the King?" "Yes,
sire." "Then go back, freely, as is right." The men returned to the castle, and the next day its garrison
surrendered.

Richard spent the next day visiting Sherwood Forest, which he had never seen before, and declared
that it "pleased him well." In the old Robin Hood
stories we hear how he came upon the outlaws and
disclosed his identity to them, just as he had to the
rebel envoys on the day before, and how Robin
Hood knelt before him and was pardoned. There
could well be truth in it. It depends mainly on

whether our Robin Hood is the one mentioned in the official records of 1230 (*Robertus Hood fugitivus*), who could have been alive at this time, or the one serving King Eward II in 1323, as some people think. But if Robin Hood *was* in Sherwood that day, it is very likely that he remembered how Richard had relaxed the forest laws and promised pardon to outlaws, in which case it would have been obvious common sense to stage a meeting as the royal party rode through the greenwood.

If there were troubles to settle in England, there were far more serious ones to attend to in his French domains. Five weeks after his visit to Sherwood, Richard took ship from Portsmouth. Though he lived for another five years, he never saw England again.

Those five years were spent in restoring his authority over his French vassals and in fighting King Philip, now his open enemy. He was hoping all the time that, once these troubles were over, he would be able to keep his vow and return to the Holy Land. It was during this period that he showed his genius as a castle builder—and, incidentally, his ability to learn from his ingenious Saracen enemies—by raising the majestic stronghold of Chateau-Gaillard to defend his Norman boundaries against Philip. "How beautiful is my one-year-old daughter!" he exclaimed as he gazed upon the finished fortress after twelve months of toil.

He was never to have a daughter of flesh and blood. He had been rejoined by Berengaria—whatever trouble had arisen between them was smoothed away—but although she remained with him to the day of his death, they never had any children.

His end came at the siege of Chalus, a paltry little fortress involved in a trivial quarrel. Richard was wounded by a crossbowman, who, having lost his father and two brothers in wars against Richard, had waited patiently for the chance of revenge. The wound led to blood poisoning, and on April 6, 1199, with his mother and probably Berengaria also at his bedside, Richard's fierce heart ceased to beat. He was not yet forty-two—but in one sense he was ageless. For as long as the tales of chivalry are told, he will have his place among the immortals.

THE YEARS BETWEEN

1199-1600

A gulf of four centuries lies between the first Rich-ard and the first Charles. Into those years fall many of the best-known events and personalities in Eng-lish history.

There is first the slow flowering of the Middle Ages—not only the blood-spotted glories of the Black Prince and Henry V of Agincourt but the de-velopment of a civilization that has left its traces to-day in hundreds of exquisite churches and cathe-drals, in wood carvings and alabaster statues, wall paintings and manuscript books, and not least in the poems of Chaucer, the tales of Malory, the early Bi-ble translations of Wycliffe and others.

Then comes the sixteenth century, the age of the remarkable Tudor family—Henry VII, Henry VIII, his much-married son, and the three grandchildren, Edward VI, Mary I, and Elizabeth I, absolute mon-archs of the pattern then spreading in Europe. Now

England is touched by the spirit of the Renaissance. A new, more modern culture sprouts from the dead autumn leaves of the medieval period. The country looks different: baronial castles give place to mansions and manors, flower beds blossom in dried moats and former courtyards, the peasant's hut is now a comfortable cottage, the hunting forests have shrunk before the advance of the plow. It is the age of Shakespeare, Raleigh, and Drake.

Men's minds have changed. England has seen the Reformation and the dissolution of the monasteries. She has become a Protestant nation, though many cling to the old religion and not all the others agree about the new. Religion is a burning issue, mixed up with politics. Men are prepared to fight and die for it. Such a man is Charles Stuart, soon to take the stage.

†††

CHARLES: THE SAD

CAVALIER

He was born in Scotland, spoke with a strong Scots accent all his life, and preferred Scotsmen to Englishmen around him. Yet it was his fate to see Scotland only once or twice after his babyhood, to lead his troops against a Scottish army, and at the last to be sold by Scotsmen to his English enemies.

Charles entered the world on November 19, 1600, at Dunfermline Castle near the Firth of Forth, sixteen miles from Edinburgh. Here, too, his father had been born before him—King James VI of Scotland, soon to be King James I of England. It was a spot famous in Scottish history. In the great abbey nearby lay such national heroes as Malcolm Canmore and Robert the Bruce.

His early memories of his parents were sketchy. He was a delicate child, and it was thought best to leave him in the country quiet of Dunfermline while they were holding court in their palace at

Holyrood. He saw more of the doctors and nurses appointed to look after him, and of Lord Fife, his official guardian. But when his father did visit him, he was aware of a fattish man whose clothing was so quilted and padded that he seemed even fatter, and so soft and yielding and puddingy to the childish embrace that it was sometimes hard to believe that there was a real man inside the cushioning. When the man bent to kiss his son, he was found to have a thin, straggly beard and wet lips. It was noticeable, too, that James washed even less—much less—than most people in that far from particular age.

Charles probably enjoyed his mother's kisses more. The Queen—Anne of Denmark—was a gay, featherbrained creature with a passion for acting and dancing. What need for brains there? Had not her husband enough for both? But James was so solemn with his learning—was he not to go down in history as "the wisest fool in Christendom"? The little boy would not have been alone in his taste if he had preferred the laughing gaiety of the Scandinavian girl. He, too, though, had a strong dash of his father's solemnity.

He had a brother, Henry, six years older, and a sister, Elizabeth, four years older than himself. Henry he must have admired and envied—everyone admired Henry, so healthy and good-looking and full of life. And his sister had all the same charm and high spirits. Charles' love for Elizabeth was the strongest emotion in his early life.

Soon after his second birthday, he lost—for the time being—these lively companions. He was too

young to understand just why they had vanished
from his daily life. The Queen of England, that
wicked old woman who had once cut off the head of
his grandmother, Mary Queen of Scots, had died at
last. A gentleman, Sir Robert Carey, had galloped
northwards at breakneck speed to offer James the
sapphire ring he had snatched from the still-warm
finger of the dead Elizabeth. It was a long-awaited
sign. James had his plans made to take over his inheritance. He started south for England with his
wife. Soon Henry and Elizabeth were summoned to
join their parents. But it was thought that Charles, a
sickly, backward child, unable either to walk or to
talk properly, was better left in Scotland.

It was more than a year (in July, 1604) before the
doctors said he was fit for the long journey. The little
boy traveled in a closed litter. Over the appalling
roads of the seventeenth century even an ordinary
traveler took more than a week. It was probably
longer than that before the litter halted in the
courtyard of an inn at Northampton, the curtains
were pulled back, and the little prince was lifted out
onto the cobbles, where his father, whom he had almost forgotten, stood ready to meet him.

Poor Charles! No one looking at that puny manikin, stumbling both in walk and speech, could have
foreseen that he would live to wear more royal dignity than almost any other British sovereign before
or after him.

"Manikin" is a fair description, for, like all the
children of the period, Charles was enveloped in
heavy garments reaching to his ankles. There were

no distinct children's clothes as we understand them. When he first arrived in England he was probably still wearing a full-length coat, hiding undercoats or "petticoats." But very soon, at about six, he would be solemnly "breeched"—that is, fitted by the tailor with a complete adult suit in miniature, with coat and waistcoat (and, if need be, corsets to make them fit well), and even a plumed hat and tiny sword.

Henry was rather unkind about Charles' weak legs. When he was king himself, he said, he would make "Baby Charles" his Archbishop of Canterbury. Then the legs could always be hidden by flowing robes. As he said this, Henry picked up the archbishop's hat (for the actual archbishop was at that moment in the next room with their father) and clapped it on his brother's head. Charles was so furious that he flung the hat on the floor and stamped on it, and it was all Henry could do to rescue it in a fit state for its owner to wear again.

Charles' temper was understandable. He was always being made to feel inferior. Those wretched legs! His father had wanted to make him wear irons to strengthen them. His new governess had saved him from that misery. Lady Carey, wife of that Sir Robert Carey who had posted northwards with the sapphire ring, had taken over the care of Charles, and she flew to his defense like a hen with one chick. No irons, no operation on the tongue to cure his defective speech! James gave way. For the next seven years Charles lived under Lady Carey's kindly wing, first in one of the King's country houses near London, then in another.

Year by year he grew stronger. He never lost a slight hesitation in his speech, but it never hindered him in his public duties. He would never have the athletic grace of Henry, but at least he could move across a hall without his father's ungainly waddle. And he could dance well enough, too.

When he was ten, he danced in a masque at court. It was called the *Masque of the Rivers* and had been especially written for the celebrations when Henry was created Prince of Wales.

Masques were what the Queen loved. The dances, the tableaux, the music, the lighting effects could be enjoyed with less mental effort than the play. Even Shakespeare had taken note of the changed tastes and fashions at court: he had just included a masque in his latest comedy, *The Tempest,* and now would trouble to write no more.

The Queen herself took part in the *Masque of the Rivers.* She was Tethys, the sea goddess, with a sea-shell helmet and a blue robe laced with silver seaweed. Elizabeth sat at her feet looking very lovely as the Nymph of the Thames. Charles himself was arrayed in a green tunic sprigged with flowers, and wore wings of silver gauze. He had an important part. First he had to lead a *corps de ballet* of twelve nobly born little girls. Then he had to present his father, in the audience, with Neptune's golden trident, and his brother with a jeweled sword and the scarf their mother had embroidered for the occasion.

Charles got through his part without mishap, and to great applause. His legs could not be so bad after all! But the feeling of inferiority was by now too deeply implanted for it to be removed by any suc-cess. All his life, Charles was happier in the saddle than on foot.

Riding! His eyes would light up at the thought. On horseback he was equal to anyone, even Henry. Henry loved a good gallop but was not a really keen huntsman. Charles himself developed a lifelong pas-sion for the sport, and in time became one of the finest horsemen in the kingdom. Riding after his hounds, he knew none of the fears and doubts that haunted him at other times. Once, as a man, gallop-ing through that New Forest that had already claimed one English king as victim, he plunged into a deep bog. The horse was drowned. Charles was not pulled out until the ooze was sucking at the lace about his throat. Yet no sooner was he safe than he demanded a change of clothes and a fresh mount, on which he thundered away in quest of the stag. In the saddle Charles was a different person.

He had a wistful longing to shine as a man of ac-tion. Henry, of course, one day would be King of England; Charles did not grudge him that. Despite Henry's teasing, he grudged him nothing. Had he not once written to Henry: "Sweet, sweet brother, I will give anything that I have to you, both my horse, and my books and my fowling-pieces, and my cross-bows, or anything that you would have . . ."? Yes, Henry would be King Henry the Ninth of England.

Elizabeth would be a German princess: her engagement would shortly be announced to Frederick, the Elector Palatine. But what would he himself become?

Certainly not Archbishop of Canterbury—sincere and devout though he was in his prayers! He wanted to be a soldier. Why not a soldier of fortune serving some great foreign power such as the Republic of Venice? Many a man of noble blood had served under the Venetian flag, like Othello in Shakespeare's play. The pale Scots boy dreamed his own dream of

"battles, sieges, fortunes . . .
Of moving accidents by flood and field;
Of hair-breadth scapes i' th' imminent deadly breach;
Of being taken by the insolent foe . . ."

Suddenly, two weeks before his twelfth birthday, the dream was shattered. Forever, it seemed to him. He was spared the foreknowledge that, in a terrible way, its fulfillment was only postponed.

London was buying fireworks and heaping up bonfires ready for Guy Fawkes Night. It was just seven years since the discovery of the Gunpowder Plot, which was to have blown up his father and Henry and both Houses of Parliament. And now Henry, who had escaped that death, was stricken with a mysterious fever. He lay delirious at a country house in Essex. Even his father was dissuaded by the doctors from entering the sickroom. He gave orders that no other member of the family should run the risk, but Elizabeth, with her usual spirit, disobeyed her father and went down to Essex in disguise, only to be recognized and turned away. On November 6, Henry, Prince of Wales and darling of the English people, died. The pale, sad-eyed younger brother knew then that, if he lived long enough, it was he who must follow his father as King of England.

Charles knew what it meant to be a king. No son of James I could be in any doubt about it. Charles had heard his father on a great number of topics—on the wickedness of tobacco smoking and the obstinacy of Puritans and the impertinence of Parliaments—but on no subject more eloquently than that of kingly rights. In a speech to Parliament, just before Henry's death, James had declaimed in his broad Scots accent: "The state of monarchy is the supreme thing upon earth. Kings are God's lieutenants upon earth and sit upon God's throne. As to dispute what God may do is blasphemy, so it is treason in subjects to dispute what a king may do in the height of his power. I will not be contented that my power be disputed on."

God's lieutenant. . . . That was what he, too, must be. Never in his life did Charles budge from the teaching his father had laid down. A king could not be wrong. However humble and modest he might be as a private individual, a king must never yield an inch of ground to his subjects. That was his duty, not only to himself but to his successors on the throne and to the divine power that had set him there.

Little did James guess that in laying down this dogma he was sharpening the ax for his own son's neck and opening up a road that would lead his grandson, James II, into hopeless exile.

Charles was lonelier after Henry's death. Elizabeth's engagement had been announced soon afterwards, and soon his adored sister departed overseas to begin her new life. Charles never saw her again. The royal family was now quite broken up. The King no longer cared for the Queen and seldom spent any time with her. He preferred the company of his young noblemen—especially the brilliant George Villiers, whom he was rapidly promoting through all the successive grades of the peerage. The Queen was often ill; she could no longer shine like a sun in the middle of her court, but spent more and more time quietly in the country. Charles could not visit her as often as he would have wished. He had had to take over Henry's former home, St. James's Palace, for even a boy prince must have his separate household, and there he lived, a stone's throw from his father at Whitehall Palace, with his own host of officers and attendants.

The court life disgusted him, with its gambling and its immorality, its cruel gossip and its shameless self-seeking. He might have echoed the lines of Walter Raleigh—Raleigh, the prisoner in the Tower, who had been Henry's friend and hero and was now soon to die as the victim of their father's meanness:

"Go tell the Court it glows
And shines like rotten wood . . ."

Charles turned from the uncleanness of Whitehall. He trained his body like a modern schoolboy, taking daily runs. He insisted on mastering great chargers that were thought too strong and fiery for him. And he mastered them. He rode in the courtyard, for the old medieval tournaments still lingered as a pictur- esque survival. He played tennis.

He never grew tall. That was another reason why he felt more confident when he was on horseback. But he was good-looking—people said he took after his mother. His forehead was high, his hair lightish brown, his dark eyes certainly more thoughtful and melancholy than the Queen's. Later, a neat pointed beard was to give an added length and sharpness to his face—or a foxiness, his enemies might say.

When he was sixteen he was made Prince of Wales. He was glad that his father was sufficiently pleased with him to confer the title. He might not be *worthy* to follow poor Henry and wear the os- trich plumes, but at least the King did not think him hopelessly unfit.

Charles was hungry for his father's approval and bitterly jealous of the young men like Villiers, now Marquis of Buckingham, so much more showy than himself, who had first claim on the King's company. He had several childish quarrels with Buckingham. Once, in the gardens of Greenwich Palace, he lay in wait for him where there was a waterspout con- cealed among the trees (a form of practical joke highly popular in the seventeenth century) and, suddenly turning on the tap, drenched his rival. James was so furious that he boxed his ears soundly for it. But Buckingham showed great tact and gradually won over the sulky boy. In time he became the closest friend—almost the only close friend—Charles ever had.

That friendship was soon to be needed. At eighteen Charles lost his mother. She died at Hampton Court. He had hurried to her bedside, hardly realizing how ill she was. His father, callous and indifferent, did not interrupt his hunting at Newmarket.

That was the year before the *Mayflower* sailed from Plymouth carrying Puritans who preferred the unknown perils of America to the Church of England discipline demanded by the King. Men were prepared to emigrate for freedom, but they did not yet think of fighting for it . . .

Charles was twenty, twenty-one, twenty-two. . . . He was shy and so far had shown little interest in girls, but it was time to think of a wife for him. There was talk of a French princess, but peace-loving James was more interested in strengthening friendship with the old enemy, Spain. The Spanish ambassador, Gondomar, was a typical grandee, haughty, cultured, superb. He charmed not only James but Charles, too. He dropped hints about a possible marriage with the Infanta of Spain. Charles was flattered and grew interested. Gondomar gave him the princess' colors, sent specially from Madrid, and Charles wore them on his helmet in the tilt yard. But time passed and the matter went no further, as Gondomar did not intend it to. He was merely using the suggestion as a decoy, to keep England friendly.

Charles and Buckingham—"Steenie," as the King called him—were not satisfied to let the matter drop. Why should they not go to Madrid, suggested Steenie, and woo this Spanish beauty? They could travel incognito; it would never do for them to go officially, but for that very reason it would be a delightful adventure. James heard of the idea, laughed, and forbade it, but if he did not take it seriously, neither did the young men pay too much attention to his ban.

They went ahead with their plans in secret. One Monday in February they asked the King for two days' leave of absence from court to go hunting.

"See that you be with us on Friday night," said James.

"Sire," said Buckingham, "if we should stay a day or two longer, I hope your Majesty will pardon us?"

"Well, well," murmured James and, possibly guessing what was afoot, asked no more questions.

They set off with three or four attendants the next morning. Charles and Steenie had donned false beards and muffled themselves in vast riding coats. One of the beards fell off as they clattered through Gravesend. It was carried to the local mayor, who, suspecting treason, sent an officer to overtake the mysterious strangers. Steenie dealt with the officer with his usual charm and skill and sent him back with a promise to keep his mouth shut. Taking a roundabout route, they made for Dover, where there were more awkward questions to answer before they could sail. They both were sick crossing the Channel, but at last they landed safely in France and started posthaste for Paris. Steenie fell off four times on the way.

They stayed five days in Paris and wrote a reassuring letter to the King in London. Thus, when they reached Madrid, the news had gone ahead of them, and they were given a public welcome. The Spaniards were polite, but they avoided any definite promises. Charles was not allowed to meet, or even to get a close view of, the princess he hoped to marry. This was not England, he was told, but Spain. The Infanta led a secluded life, like any other well-bred girl. Charles did not actually serenade her, but he tried other means of seeing what she was like. He climbed a tree so that he could look over her garden wall and steal a glimpse of her, and, as the weeks passed without any clear progress, he had the best spyglasses in London sent out to him, to focus upon her too-distant charms.

Meanwhile, in England, there was strong public feeling against the match. England wanted no Spanish queen. The summer passed. James was ill and wanted his son home. Steenie, who had left a young wife and child of his own behind, was tired of the Madrid adventure. It had gone far, far beyond a joke. . . . An English fleet was sent to bring the Prince of Wales home, with or without a bride, in a manner fitting to his rank. The Prince came home without—and the delight of the English people more than made up for the failure of his wooing. Charles was welcomed with bell ringing and bonfires. He was dumfounded to find himself for the first time in his life (and, as it proved, the last) a genuinely popular hero. And all because he had come home without the girl.

Just over a year later, in the spring of 1625, James died. For a week Charles shut himself up in his apartments. When he came out he looked paler than ever, and sadder, for despite all his father's faults, he had deeply loved the grotesque old king. In a long black cloak he walked across the park to Whitehall, henceforth to be the main setting of his life—and, had he but known it, his death.

"Charles, by the Grace of God, King . . ."

The heralds' formula was no string of empty words to the new sovereign. Charles felt he *was* King by the grace of God. He was the Lord's anointed, "God's lieutenant," as his father had said to Parliament years before. His whole position rested on the divine right of kings.

In that spirit he began by cleaning up the life of the court. There was to be an end of the bad old ways, "the beastly delights" (as one witness termed them) that had shocked him as a child. There must be decency and order, respect for religion.

"If he will not come to my prayers," cried Charles when one courtier avoided the daily service, "let him get out of my house!"

On the other hand, nobody was sent away from court if his conduct was satisfactory. It had been the normal practice for a new sovereign to dismiss the former officers and hand out their posts to his own favorites. Charles felt this was unfair.

Whitehall was easy to control; Parliament was a

different matter. When he opened his first Parliament at Oxford he received an unpleasant shock.

Hitherto, a new sovereign had been granted the revenues known as "tunnage and poundage" for the rest of his life. To Charles they were voted only for the coming year.

There were men in Parliament who did not share his belief in the divine right of kings. They believed that kings and peoples should work in partnership, both under the law, and that it was as wrong for the king to break that partnership as for his people to do so. But there was only one way to control him, and that was to keep a tight hold on the purse strings.

If a king had money, he could govern indefinitely without troubling to call Parliament. Even the popular Elizabeth had avoided calling together her "faithful Commons" except when she was driven to it by want of money. In 1603 Parliament had made the mistake of voting tunnage and poundage to James for life. They did not mean to repeat their mistake in 1625. There was nothing personal against Charles in what they did; they were simply seizing a chance that might not offer itself for another half century, should he live to a ripe old age.

But to Charles it was intensely personal. One of the first things for which he needed money was military aid to his sister's husband in Bohemia. Parliament's act was a blow at his beloved sister as well as an insult to his royal dignity. He accepted the situation because he could do nothing else, but he noted his enemies and remembered them.

He had other things, too, to think of in those first months of his reign. It was a king's duty to marry and have children to inherit the throne. England had gone through enough doubt and anxiety under the unmarried Queen Elizabeth and the childless monarchs before her. Now that he was King, Charles must settle the marriage question.

His bride was already chosen. She had been chosen and approved before his father's death, and it was time to proceed with the wedding.

Charles was to marry Henrietta Maria, sister of the French king and daughter of the gay and dashing Henry of Navarre. If Charles had ever seen her—which was just possible, when he visited the French court incognito during his five-day visit to Paris—he had no distinct memory of her. She was a Roman Catholic, but his people were far more ready to accept a French princess of that religion than the Infanta of Spain. Besides, she was little more than a child and could be molded into a suitable Queen of England.

The marriage took place by proxy before she left Paris. Charles could not leave the country to fetch her, but the court moved down to Canterbury to await her arrival. When news came that she had landed at Dover, he mounted his horse impulsively and galloped over the Kentish Downs to welcome her.

He arrived unheralded, without ceremony, a pale young man of twenty-four in a plain riding suit. At the best of times he was simple in his dress. After the resplendence of Elizabeth and the balloonlike bombast of his father's clothes, Charles made a dark, elegant figure, lit by small touches such as his silver cane, an occasional diamond, or the Mechlin lace at his collar.

Henrietta was dressing. He had to wait. After a few minutes he saw her coming down the long hall toward him—a flushed, eager girl of fifteen. She knelt and kissed his hand. He raised her and kissed her over and over again. Then, at arm's length, they stared and smiled at each other. She was *petite,* yes, but a little taller than the ambassador had told him. Reading the look in his eyes, she laughed.

"I stand upon my own feet, sir! I have no art to help me—I am neither taller nor shorter than this!"

She came only to his shoulder, and he was not a big man. But what they lacked in inches they made up in true royalty.

They went in to a good dinner of pheasant and venison. Her confessor—she had brought with her a numerous train of Capuchin monks as well as her French servants—reminded her that it was a fast day. Henrietta proceeded to enjoy the pheasant and the venison with a healthy fifteen-year-old appetite sharpened by sea air. There were times when she was meek and obedient to her priests and other times when she flouted them. The very marriage itself had taken place without waiting for the Pope's dispensation, and she had been told to wait sixteen days at Amiens by way of penance, but she had been impatient. How could it be wrong to hasten to the man who was now her lawful husband? Skillfully avoiding the Pope's representative, Henrietta had sailed straight for England—and here she was.

They entered London by boat; the Thames was a better highway for a State entrance than any of the narrow streets ashore. They both wore green and stood beneath the canopy of the royal barge, for it had just been raining heavily. Now the June sky was brightening, the jumbled, crooked roofs of London shone wetly, the houses on the bridge were black with tiny figures, the gray ramparts of the Tower flared and thundered with saluting cannon. The twinkling river behind them was thronged with boats of every type, each one packed to the water-line with cheering, waving Londoners. Apart from the official procession of barges, there were a thousand boats jostling their way upstream behind the bridal pair.

What was Charles feeling? He was touched and charmed by this kitten standing at his side. She was like his own mother in some ways—in her liveliness and frivolity, her lack of intellectual interests, her enthusiasm for masques and entertainments. She would be a queen of similar pattern, perhaps better. She had more sense of dignity, for all her childishness. He could not see her upsetting people and making a fool of herself, as his mother had once done, by getting herself up, and her ladies, as blackamoors for a court entertainment. She had the inherited instincts of a French princess to help her there. Yes, he could safely leave her to run the social life of the court, to preside over all the gaieties and follies that bored him but seemed unavoidable.

But he was not in love with her, and it was a long time before real love came.

She vexed him by preferring her own French ladies to the English ones provided to attend her— yet she had some excuse, since the English language was unknown to her. She angered him more by her lack of respect for his own religion; she behaved as though it were not a religion at all, and her French monks encouraged her. Once (when he himself was away) she and her ladies flounced through the assembled courtiers in the middle of their Church of England service, and then came back again, a few minutes later, chattering noisily. There were continual troubles. Worst of all, she could not be crowned Queen: she would not agree to a Protestant archbishop, and England would not agree to a Catholic, so when Charles' coronation took place, his wife could do no more than look down on the procession from a window, like any other woman in London.

If Charles was gloomy and worried, Henrietta was still more unhappy. She could not understand this cold, reserved man who had married her. Did he know the meaning of love? He would light up with some enthusiasm if it was a question of horses or oil paintings—yet did he really love *them,* or did he merely use the horses and collect the paintings? He was said to have such taste. . . . Oh, for a little less taste, sighed Henrietta, and a little more warm emotion! At Christmas, bored and rebellious, she enjoyed a brief hour of revolt, muffling herself up like an ordinary London girl and slipping away into the crowded streets to see the shops. After a time she was recognized and had to make a hurried escape. Charles would not have approved of such goings-on. Of course, it had been all right for Charles and his precious Steenie to go incognito to Madrid!

They lived this strained, awkward life together for nearly a year. Then, one afternoon, Charles came into her apartments and found some of her French gentlemen playing the fool with more familiarity than was proper in the Queen's presence. There was a sudden hush. Seeing the thunder cloud in the King's face, the girl hastily changed her own smile to a more disapproving expression. Charles said nothing. He took her hand and led her coldly from the room. When they reached his own apartments he turned the key behind them and faced her.

It had to stop, he told her. These Frenchmen must go, bag and baggage. Men, women, priests, the whole pack of them! She could keep her old nurse and her favorite dresser. The chefs could stay—they could do no harm in the kitchens. The rest must leave the palace now, this very moment, and they could lodge elsewhere until their journey to France could be arranged.

Henrietta forgot she was a Queen of England and a princess of France. She stormed and wept and screamed. When Charles went out, turning the key on her, she broke the window with her fist. The expelled French attendants looked up and saw her as they were being driven out of the palace by the yeomen of the guard.

When she recovered from her rage and her old

retinue had left the country, Henrietta discovered that they had gone off with most of her own clothes. Perhaps, after all, Charles had been right in some of the things he had said about them! Perhaps, after all, Charles was a better man than she had suspected?

From that time the royal marriage entered a happier, warmer stage.

In after years, Charles' reign was to be remembered as the era of the civil war. It is often forgotten that most of his reign was outwardly peaceful and that he ruled for seventeen years before there was talk of civil war, and before Englishmen divided into royalist "Cavaliers" and Parliamentarian "Roundheads"—the latter being scornfully so-called because of the short haircut they preferred.

Yet much happened in those seventeen years. More English emigrants sailed westwards to colonize America. Maryland was founded and named in honor of the Queen. Harvard was established, later to grow into the great American university. And eastwards the merchants of the East India Company opened the trading post which was to become Calcutta, and laid the foundations of Britain's power in Asia. Charles built up the navy again, which his father had allowed to decay through too much economy. The *Sovereign of the Seas*, launched in 1637, was a great advance in ship design. Charles was criticized for levying the tax called "ship money"— but mainly by people who lived at a safe distance inland. Coast dwellers were glad of protection against the Algerian pirates who, at the height of their power, came raiding even into the English Channel.

Meanwhile, ashore, much was happening, too. While the Dutchman Van Dyck painted Charles, his family, and the aristocracy of England, his fellow countryman Vermuyden was draining the Fens and creating a great new tract of fertile farmland. Inigo Jones, the architect, was still alive and at work, nor was he the only man who could build: at Oxford, an unknown craftsman named Smith created the exquisite fan vaulting over the staircase to Christ Church hall—not only one of the finest specimens of the style in the world but, most curiously, two hundred years later than the age to which that style belonged. Many a time was Charles to pass and repass beneath that vaulting when Christ Church became his wartime home and he kept state in the noble hall at the top of those stairs. But the humble Smith's fan vaulting was unusual in imitating bygone fashions. The new buildings of Charles' reign had their own individuality. It is to be seen in other Oxford colleges, notably in the second quadrangle of St. John's, built by Archbishop Laud, and at Cambridge, in the palatial splendor of Clare, and in country houses such as Raynham Hall in Norfolk.

The other arts flourished. Charles himself was the greatest art collector among all the English kings. There was much singing and playing, in and out of church: England, so musical under the Tudors, continued musical until the disapproving Puritans disbanded the choirs, pulled the organs out of the churches, banned Christmas carols and May Day dances, and frowned on most other forms of merry-making.

As for literature, John Milton was writing the masque of *Comus* and the lament for *Lycidas*. Herrick and Herbert, Lovelace and Suckling were pouring out shorter poems that still are in every anthology. John Donne's strange, passionate verses, written many years earlier, were first published in 1633, just after his death. His biography was being written by his friend, Izaak Walton, a self-educated Fleet Street ironmonger, later to win fame as the author of *The Compleat Angler*. Sir Thomas Browne wrote *Religio Medici*. Ben Jonson and some of the other Elizabethan and Jacobean playwrights were still working for the six theaters that were now open in London, but younger dramatists such as Massinger, Ford, and Shirley were moving up into their places. The stage was active, but the new plays were only second-rate, as in Victorian England. Henrietta Maria, like the previous queen, preferred masques —not unnaturally, for both women were foreigners and could never have grasped fully the rich spate of words poured out by a Shakespeare or a Marlowe. So the theater, lacking the encouragement of court, catered to the less cultured playgoer.

Science was beginning to move out of the realm of superstition. Men were beginning to experiment, to correspond and exchange theories. Soon—in 1645, the year that the battle of Naseby was fought —they were to band themselves together more formally into "the Invisible College," which would develop later into the Royal Society. Men with inquiring minds were ready to look back as well as forwards, and Charles himself patronized archaeology as a study "very useful to the general good of the State and Commonwealth."

There were changes in everyday life. Newspapers began in the first year of his reign, though their freedom of speech was strictly limited. The sedan chair appeared, soon to be followed by the stagecoach.

Altogether, those seventeen years from 1625 to 1642 were not empty for England.

Nor were they empty years for the King and Queen. Gradually their state marriage became an affectionate personal one. Though they had the grief of losing their first baby at birth, and later two others, as was a common misfortune in those days, they had other children who grew up into a happy family—the boys and girls who were one day to be Charles II, Mary of Orange (mother of William III), James II, Elizabeth (Queen of Bohemia), and Henry, Duke of Gloucester, who died young, of smallpox, in the year of the Restoration. Later still, in 1644, came Charles II's favorite sister, Henrietta, nicknamed "Minette." There was no banishing of these children to guardians and governesses away from court. Charles was devoted to them, supervising their lessons and forgetting his grave dignity to take part in their games.

The Queen had no reason now to be jealous of Steenie. Buckingham was stabbed by a discontented officer at Portsmouth, and died instantly. The news was brought to Charles as he knelt in chapel. He waved the messengers aside and continued in prayer without any sign of emotion, but, the service ended, he shut himself away in a day-long agony of grief. He never had so close a friend again. His advisers became Archbishop Laud and Lord Strafford, but neither took the place of the gay Steenie, with whom he had once ridden out along the road to Spain.

Though the civil war did not break out until 1642, all those previous seventeen years were the preparation for it. Parliament was determined to control the country, Charles was equally determined to keep his "divine rights" intact for the kings who would follow him. Step by step, from the Petition of Right to the Grand Remonstrance, Parliament pushed him back. Step by step Charles retreated, until he felt the wall behind him and knew he could retreat no more. He was no tyrant by nature. He was ready to give way, for the sake of peace, on a number of issues. But there came a day when he knew he must fight, and another day when he knew he must die, rather than surrender on the main question.

Parliament sent Laud to prison and Strafford to the block. They had been Charles' loyal ministers, but he would not provoke the coming revolution by trying to save them. Full of remorse, deeply ashamed, he left the two men to their fate.

He tried to force the Prayer Book on Scotland, which had kept a separate Parliament and which he governed through a secretary of state, hardly crossing the border himself except for his Scottish coronation. The Scots rebelled and swore the Covenant to resist his form of religion. They invaded England. Charles had the pain of marching against his fellow countrymen, and then the humiliation of having to give way to their demands.

It was Henrietta Maria, unused to the English and the Scots alike, accustomed only to the high-handed methods of foreign kings, who was continually goading him to defy his subjects. And it was Parliament's bold proposal to impeach her, to put the King's own wife on trial for her actions, that proved the last straw.

What follows is a familiar story. Henrietta taunted Charles. "Go, poltroon, pull these rogues by the ears—or see my face no more!" His pride stung, Charles strode across to Westminster with his eleven-year-old son excitedly trotting at his heels, his nephew Prince Rupert (Elizabeth's dashing son), and five hundred soldiers at his back. He burst into the House of Commons and tried to arrest the five members responsible for this insult to the Queen. If he had succeeded, the results would have been serious for him. But he failed—"the birds had flown"—and he was left to look ridiculous, which was worse.

That was January, 1642. In February, Henrietta left England, making Charles promise to yield no more to Parliament until she returned. She was taking their daughter Mary to Holland. The rest of the children stayed with their father. For the next six months Charles and his enemies gathered their forces for the battle that was now certain, but which neither wished to begin. On August 22, on a hillock outside Nottingham Castle, Charles raised his standard with the device GIVE CAESAR HIS DUE. The civil war had begun.

There is no space here to tell the story of the English civil war. It was a long-drawn-out affair, with neither side strong enough for some years to deliver a knockout blow. It began with a drawn battle at Edgehill, followed, after many skirmishes and sieges large and small, by the famous Roundhead victories at Marston Moor and Naseby. Prince Rupert proved the outstanding general on the Royalist side, while for Parliament Oliver Cromwell came gradually to the fore. His nickname, "Old Ironsides," was intended to apply to all the new troops he raised and trained in his "New Model Army." It was their iron discipline, backed by their religious and political enthusiasm, that was to defeat the King in the end.

When not riding with his troops, Charles spent most of those years at the royalist headquarters in Oxford. Wolsey's magnificent college, Christ Church, became his palace. The Cavalier minority held their own "parliament" in its hall, and the chapel, already doing double duty as Oxford Cathedral, became also the King's place of worship. Council meetings were held at Oriel College nearby, and Henrietta, when she ran the gantlet of the Roundheads and returned from abroad, had her apartments over the archway at Merton, with a private way made for her into Christ Church through Corpus Christi, the small college sandwiched between.

As a rest from cares of state, Charles found delight in the quiet gardens of the university or amid the bookshelves of the Bodleian Library.

But the war, after beginning well for Charles, went badly. First there was the defeat at Marston Moor. Oxford became less safe, and Henrietta was sent down into the West Country. Charles rode out with her the first few miles, and their farewells were made in the little Berkshire town of Abingdon. Later Henrietta went to France—she was ill and her nerve was breaking—and so she never saw his face again.

Cromwell's triumph at Naseby broke the main Cavalier army. But Charles remembered that he was still King of England, not a defeated foreign general. His enemies were not united. Parliament was jealous of its own army leaders, and the Scots army, brought into England as their allies, had a hand of its own to play. Charles was like a man whose sword is broken but whose wits are still sharp. Might he not continue the struggle by political bargaining?

The Scots seemed his best hope. A month before Oxford surrendered to the Roundheads, a disguised king slipped out of the city before dawn and hurried northwards to the Scots army in Nottinghamshire. There followed nine months of weary conferences. At the finish, the Scots cautiously decided they would strike a better bargain with Parliament. They sold Charles for £200,000, which was the amount of their back pay handed over to them by the Roundheads.

That was January, 1647. For the next two years

Charles was kept prisoner in various places and under different conditions. Sometimes he was closely watched and strictly confined; at others he was treated with great respect and allowed freedom for exercise and amusement. At one stage he was able to hunt and play tennis, and have his younger children, James, Elizabeth, and Henry, lodging nearby. Once, in Hampshire, he escaped and was at large for some time, trying to get a boat to the Channel Isles, but he was recaptured before he could do so. A second attempt at escape, from Carisbrooke Castle on the Isle of Wight, failed at the last moment because Charles, small though he was, could not squeeze his shoulders through the narrow window of his room. When a third chance of freedom came it was too late: by then Charles had given his parole, and though an easy means of escape was open, he refused to break his royal word of honor.

In 1648 the war flared up again. There were Cavalier risings in Wales and Essex, and the Scots, switching sides, came over the border again—only to be smashed by Cromwell at the battle of Preston Moor. In a sense it was his supporters who sealed Charles' fate. The extreme Parliamentary party felt there would be no certain peace while Charles lived. It was decided to try him and put him to death.

Charles was not the only man who believed that a king could not be tried in this way and that no earthly court could sit in judgment upon him. The famous Parliamentary general, Fairfax, was only one of many sincere Roundheads who would have nothing to do with the proceedings. The trial was forced through by a ruthless and determined group, claiming to represent the people of England but actually forming only a minority of a minority of a Parliament elected (by a minority of the population) nine years earlier.

In January, 1649, Charles faced his accusers in the Great Hall of Westminster. He sat on a velvet-covered chair, a smallish, dark-clad figure, fingering a cane with a silver knob. Silvering, too, was his hair, though he was still on the young side of fifty, but few were near enough to see, for he kept his hat on, as was common indoor practice in that century. The years of care had sharpened the lines of his face.

Though he refused to plead either guilty or not guilty—since he could not agree that the trial was legal—he did not remain silent. For a whole week he stubbornly argued the point at every opportunity. No one, even his scholarly father, was better equipped by now to discuss a king's position in relation to the law and the people. And James could never have backed his learning with the courage and dignity that his son now showed on the threshold of death.

It was all to no avail. The result of the trial had been decided by his enemies even before it began. On the last day the sentence was pronounced, "that the said Charles Stuart, as a tyrant, traitor, murderer, and a public enemy, shall be put to death by the severing his head from his body." Charles made a last appeal for the right to speak, was refused, and was hustled away by the pikemen guarding him. "I am not suffered for to speak," he said quietly. "Expect what justice *other* people will have!" There was a sedan chair waiting outside. The chairmen doffed their hats respectfully, but the soldiers roughly quelled this, as well as all other signs of sympathy for the prisoner.

That was Saturday. The execution was fixed for the following Tuesday morning, on a scaffold to be erected in front of Whitehall Palace. Charles spent the week end settling the small affairs of this world and preparing himself for the next. He had been allowed to have his dogs with him to the end, Gypsy the greyhound and his spaniel Rogue. They would be sent to Henrietta in France. Young Charles should have his Bible, and James a little silver sundial. James, too, was safely overseas by now; he had been spirited away by loyal friends during a carefully timed game of hide-and-seek. Elizabeth and Henry were still in London. They were brought to say good-by. There were books and trinkets for them. There were other gifts of watches, rings, and such things for his most faithful friends.

His one remaining worry was that he should not behave with proper dignity in the last awful scene on that stage lifted above the crowd at Whitehall. He was going to his death deliberately, for the things in which he sincerely believed. There had been many occasions when he could have avoided this fate, if he had been willing to give up his beliefs. But he had kept faith with his father's teaching, kept faith with his successors as yet unborn.

As a child, stammering and unsure of his steps, he had striven so hard to be worthy of his princely rank. As a boy, the younger weakly brother of the heroic Henry, he had dreamed wistfully of action and glory on distant battlefields. Now he needed a colder courage.

"Death is not terrible to me," he assured Bishop Juxon. "I bless my God, I am prepared." He was only afraid of *seeming* afraid. He put on extra clothes lest the bitter January morning should make him shiver, and the crowd not understand.

"Remember," he said quietly to the Bishop, handing him as a keepsake the silver-knobbed cane. The black-draped platform waited outside the tall window through which he must presently go. The crowd waited, among them a fifteen-year-old St. Paul's schoolboy, Samuel Pepys, who one day would recall the morning in his diary and that, less than a dozen years later, he saw the beginning of other executions at Charing Cross, "the first blood shed in revenge for the King." The troopers waited, their faces grim under the steel peaks of their helmets, ready to crush any disorder in favor of Charles.

"I go from a corruptible crown to an incorruptible one," said Charles quietly to the Bishop when the latter fumbled for words of comfort. The moment had come. Charles stepped out into the wintry air. His dignity never faltered for an instant. It was all finished very quickly. There was no cheer from the crowd, only a low gasp of horror as the executioner displayed the royal head. The Ironsides, thankful for an excuse to do something, spurred their horses forward and began roughly to break up the unresisting, quietly muttering crowd.

Charles the King was no more. But in that moment, in the hearts of many, Charles the Martyr was born.

☩ ☩ ☩ ☩ ☩

CHARLES II: KING OF
HEARTS—OR KNAVE?

A boy snatched pen and paper, signed his name at the bottom of a blank sheet, and sent it by urgent courier to England. Let Parliament fill in whatever conditions it liked, he would honor that signature. If only they would spare his father's life!

The hot-blooded human gesture (so different from what his father would have done) had no effect. While the exiles at the French court were still numbed by the pronouncement of the death sentence, there followed the almost unbelievable news that the sentence had been carried out.

King Charles was dead. A sallow, ugly boy of eighteen found his friends and companions kneeling to kiss his hand and hailing him by his new title.

King Charles the Second . . . fated to go down in history as "the merry monarch." But at that moment the grief-shattered boy could think of only one thing: revenge.

Something of his life up to that moment has been indicated in the previous chapter. The loving, but different, parents—a grave, rather cold father, and a gay, frivolous, hot-tempered mother; the happy family circle of younger brothers and sisters; the elegance of court, with its masques and music, its talk of art and architecture; the horses and hounds, the spaniels and other dogs; and then the sad changes and anxieties of the war years.

This second Charles had been born on May 29, 1630—". . . so ugly," laughed his young mother ruefully, "that I am ashamed of him." It was no doubt from her side of the family that he got his swarthy skin, just as his lazy good humor and full-blooded passions came rather from the south of France than from the north of Britain.

His first memories were of an outwardly happy England, in which only the most farseeing of men could observe the creeping shadow of the civil war. When he turned from baby's rattle to small boy's drum and hobbyhorse, few realized how soon the country would be echoing to the thunder of real drums and charging cavalry. When he was six, his big cousin Rupert, then seventeen, came over for a visit and fell in love with the country as he saw it then. Going for a last ride on the day he left, Rupert cried out that he would not mind breaking his neck, if it meant staying in England forever. Such was the sunny world of Charles' childhood.

Quaintly enough, out of all the playthings and pets at his disposal, the little prince lavished his strongest affections on a simple block of wood and insisted on taking it to bed with him as though he could not bear to sleep alone.

Like most royal children, he knew a variety of homes. Sometimes the family was at Whitehall, sometimes they went downriver to stay at Greenwich or upriver to Hampton Court; at other times they were at Windsor. When he was eight, he was solemnly created a Knight of the Garter and given his own household, with the Earl of Newcastle and the Bishop of Chichester to supervise his education. This did not mean that his parents neglected him— they kept a close watch on his upbringing, and there is still in existence a sorrowful letter from the Queen, threatening to come over herself and make him take his medicine if he would not swallow it at the Earl's bidding.

Charles liked medicine as little as do most children. A short while afterwards, when the Earl was away, he wrote him a respectful letter with all the craftiness of an eight-year-old:

"My Lord,

I would not have you take too much physic, for it does always make me worse and I think it will do the like with you. I ride every day and am ready to follow any other directions from you. Make haste to return to him that loves you.

Charles P." *

* "P" stands for Latin *princeps,* not English "prince," just as Her present Majesty's signature is "Elizabeth R." for Latin *regina,* not "Q" for England "queen."

His mother might have smiled to read that letter. It was her great concern that Charles should develop the tact and ease of manner that her husband lacked. He was to study people rather than books. The Earl of Newcastle was completely in sympathy with this idea of education. The boy's weakness at Latin did not matter. The only subject really worth hard study was history, because history taught one about men and how to handle them.

Charles' little note about the medicine shows how promising a pupil he was from the first. If the power to charm men and women were the only object of education, his early training would have been a triumphant success.

What his father most admired in Newcastle was his horsemanship. The Earl was one of the outstanding horsemen in Europe. Riding was, as the prince's letter shows, part of the daily routine. It led to a broken arm when, at eleven, he fell from his horse somewhat heavily in Hyde Park. He was never his father's equal in the saddle, but like all the Stuarts (even his learned grandfather, James) he was keenly interested in horses. But it was racing more than staghunting that appealed to him, and it was he, when he grew up, who developed Newmarket into the famous sporting center it has been ever since. One of his nicknames, "Old Rowley," was taken from a fine stallion belonging to the royal stud.

Riding was not his only exercise. Like his father, he enjoyed tennis, the strenuous indoor tennis of

those days. He fenced and danced. He was not book-
ish, but he had wide interests, as he showed later,
notably by his amateur dabblings in science. He
loved music, but his tastes were light; he preferred
a tune he could beat time to.

From an early age he showed a keen sense of
humor—if at times a rather coarse one. That humor
never deserted him, even on his deathbed.

And he was to need it in the difficult years that
now lay before him.

Charles was twelve when the civil war began in
1642.

Too young to fight yet, he stayed close at his
father's heels, as he had done on that day when they
had marched across to the House of Commons and
tried to arrest the five members. The King wanted
him under his eye. He was haunted by a fear that
the Roundheads would get hold of the boy and use
him either as a hostage or as a puppet king in opposition to himself.

Young Charles watched the first battle, Edgehill,
from the steep Warwickshire hillside above. His
little brother James was with him, and they were in
the charge of the King's doctor, the famous William
Harvey, who discovered the circulation of the blood.
Dr. Harvey sat on the grass calmly reading a book,
indifferent to the blood flowing so tragically on the
battlefield below. Only when some shots pattered
dangerously near did he jump to his feet and lead
his protesting companions farther up the hill.

Young Charles reveled in the rough fun of campaigning. He liked mixing with the common soldiers—he was never a snob—and it was noticed, with some dismay, how readily he picked up the bad language and broad jokes that were bandied around the campfires.

He spent the next year or two with his parents in Oxford. When the war took a turn for the worse and his mother went abroad, Charles was sent to Bristol for greater safety. The King had changed his mind now: it was better for the Prince of Wales to be in another place. He himself might be captured, and the boy must not be captured, too.

With the fifteen-year-old prince he sent a remarkable man, Edward Hyde. Hyde was a lawyer and a Member of Parliament. He did not believe in the divine right of kings but in a proper partnership between king and Parliament. He had voted, in his time, with the King's most bitter opponents, but when matters had come to actual warfare he had joined the royalists. The King had seen his great abilities, despite their differences of opinion. In trusting the prince to Hyde, he ensured (without realizing it) that his son would one day be welcomed back to London and would die peacefully in his bed instead of on a scaffold like himself. For two things were to make the second Charles acceptable to the people: his personality and the influence Hyde exerted on his political behavior. Not that the second Charles was ever to show any enthusiasm for Hyde's notions of working in partnership with Parliament—he liked his own way as much as ever his father had done, but at least he learned from Hyde that he could not expect to get it.

Later, Hyde was to become the Earl of Clarendon and to write the classic *History of the Rebellion.* He was also, though he did not live to see it, to become the grandfather of two English monarchs, for —flat against his wishes—his daughter married Charles' young brother James, the Duke of York, in 1660. It was their children who were later crowned as Queen Mary II and Queen Anne respectively.

All this was hidden in the future—and very well hidden—when Charles said good-by to his father and started for Bristol. With the war going so badly, no one could be sure that England would ever see another coronation at all.

Defeat followed defeat. Hyde took Charles to the Scilly Isles for safety, thence to Jersey, and at last, when the war seemed lost, to the French court at the Louvre, where his mother was living. The period of exile had begun.

There was a dramatic break in that period, when he was twenty-one.

Scotland was always the doubtful factor in the situation, for she was still an independent kingdom and her support shifted from one side to the other in the English struggle. Having handed over Charles I to the English Parliament only a few years before, the Scots now swung around to Charles II. A bargain was struck with the young exile; he landed in Scotland and was duly crowned king of that country at Scone, the traditional spot for such a ceremony. Then, with a Scottish army at his back, Charles rode southwards into England.

He had hoped that the English Cavaliers would flock to his standard, but the people were war-weary and many were disgusted by the behavior of the Scots, whom they looked upon as foreign invaders. Charles had planned a clear run through to London, for he had left Cromwell behind in Scotland with the main Roundhead army. But with only a trickle of recruits coming in, and a number of the Scots already deserting with their plunder, he realized that he would be heading for disaster. He paused, therefore, in the royalist city of Worcester, believing that with time he could build up his forces. Unfortunately that time was even more useful to the Roundheads. Cromwell was in hot pursuit. Other troops were mustering. A net of swords was closing in upon the young King.

He set up his standard in Worcester on August 22, the ninth anniversary of that fateful day when his father's had been unfurled at Nottingham. But Cromwell, too, had a taste for anniversaries. He chose to launch his attack on September 3, exactly one year after his victory over the Scots at Dunbar.

Charles knew that he was outnumbered two to one. To make up for this, he used the River Severn to divide his enemies. Having command of the city bridge, he could move his men quickly from one bank to the other as necessary. Cromwell, now moving upstream from the south, must have troops on either side; but, not having control of a bridge, he would not be able to shift reinforcements quickly from one bank to the other. Being Cromwell, however, the military genius of his age, he found his own way out of the difficulty.

Charles spent the morning of the battle riding around the lines. All was quiet. He was just finishing a meal at his headquarters when distant firing was heard. He hurried out and climbed to the top of the cathedral tower. It was then, probably, that he got his first inkling of Cromwell's daring plan. The Roundhead leader had collected twenty broad river boats and had them towed upstream against the powerful current. By laying planks across them, a pontoon bridge had been built, under the very noses of the defenders. Cromwell could now move his men to and fro as easily as Charles could—and he had twice as many to play with.

Charles did not despair. In this, his first and last battle as a commander, he showed skill as well as courage. He did not do the obvious thing. He could see that Cromwell was piling up strength on the western bank, but he did not send his own reserves scurrying over to meet them. Better, first, to strike at his enemy's weak point on the eastern bank.

Clattering down from the cathedral tower, he sprang into the saddle, gathered every available man, and led them in a furious sortie through the city gate. His bold stroke almost succeeded. The Roundheads, taken by surprise, reeled back in disorder. Only Cromwell could have saved the situation, which he did by galloping across the pontoon bridge and appearing himself to rally his stricken right wing. All that September afternoon the battle raged, until dusk came down upon the defeat of the royalists. The Scottish cavalry, having already refused to charge with the King, now fled along the darkening road to the north, leaving the infantry to save themselves if they could. And Charles, having fought gallantly throughout, found himself the most keenly hunted of all the fugitives.

The story of the next six weeks is one of the classics of "escape" literature, and it would take the whole length of this book to do justice to it.

With a reward of a thousand pounds upon his head (a vast price for those days), Charles wandered north into Shropshire and Staffordshire, then south again to Bristol, and finally eastward into Sussex.

His dark hair was clumsily cut with the aid of shears and a pudding-bowl, and his Cavalier finery was exchanged for the drab, threadbare suit of a country servant. On one occasion his borrowed shoes were so painful that he threw them away and walked in his stockings until his bleeding feet could carry him no farther. He had to skulk along hedgerows and lie hidden in the woods. One Catholic family concealed him—though he was no Catholic —in their secret priest hole. In another house he curled up to sleep in the narrow space beneath the attic floor. Most famous of all his refuges was the hollow oak at Boscobel, where, worn out by his hardships, he dozed in the arms of a comrade while the Roundhead soldiers scoured the wood around him.

At the time, even ordinary people needed passes to travel along the roads. One of the royalists, Colonel Lane, had a sister who had obtained a permit to visit a sick friend near Bristol. It was arranged that Charles should travel with her party, disguised as her manservant, "William Jackson." Jane Lane, a pretty, dark girl, was in on the secret, but even her mother did not know who "Jackson" really was. Jane rode pillion behind him, and in this fashion they traveled down the Cotswolds and into Somerset.

When they arrived there, after some narrow escapes, Charles found it still impossible to get abroad. He said a reluctant farewell to Jane and turned eastwards through Dorset and the other counties of the south coast. One set of friends passed him on to another. There was even a second spell of pillion riding, this time with the attractive Juliana Coningsby to share his horse. There were breathless moments of danger, unbearable hours of anxious waiting. And there were odd spells of relaxation (as when he went to see the wonders of Stonehenge), and incidents to tickle his ironical sense of humor. Thus, on one occasion, a drunken Cavalier spent some time vainly trying to convert the sober-looking young stranger to his own royalist opinions; and on another, when a false report had reached the district that Charles Stuart was captured and killed, Charles was able to look out of the window and

watch the villagers dancing around a bonfire to celebrate the news.

Finally, in the middle of October, a little ship was
found and he was able to flit across the Channel to
France. The brig that carried him was named, not
unsuitably, the *Surprise*.

For the next eight years Charles and his group of
faithful followers knew the real bitterness of exile.
They had hopes, still, but those hopes were dimmer
and more distant than they had been before the
adventure at Worcester.

Was there any positive certainty that they would
ever get back? Foreign governments, though horri-
fied by the death of the late King and sympathetic
to his son, were afraid of Cromwell and did not
much fancy Charles' chances against him. Under the
Lord Protector, this Commonwealth of England
was more of a force to be reckoned with than at any
time since the days of Queen Elizabeth. As always in
history, nations considered their own interests first.
For the time being, at least, they preferred not to
risk showing too much friendliness to the young
exile.

Charles and his friends were almost penniless.
The wealth of the royal family and its supporters
had long since gone to pay for the war—it had gone
up in the smoke of Marston Moor and Naseby. Gold
and silver plate had been melted down, jewelry had
been sold to the merchants of Antwerp and Amsterdam. Charles lived in shabby lodgings, ate in
cheap taverns, and went short of firewood in the

wintertime. Fortunately his good humor never deserted him. He had a taste for low life, enjoyed rubbing shoulders with the common people, and he could bear a mode of existence at which his refined father would have shuddered.

He was alive—and life was good, even under these conditions. He was young, and a pretty girl was always a pretty girl, even though one's pockets were too light to lavish presents on her.

Hyde cocked a disapproving eye on Charles' flirtations and amusements. He would have preferred the King to behave more soberly and think of his reputation, so that it would be easier some day to regain the support of the sober English people. Some of the exiles were jealous of Hyde's influence. One, trying to make mischief, burst out at the Council table: Charles should know what Hyde was saying about his behavior.

Charles laughed. "That's no news," he said, his good temper quite unruffled. "He has told me so twenty times to my face."

From eighteen onwards, he was in and out of love innumerable times. His first serious affair was with Lucy Walter, daughter of a Cavalier fugitive and described as "a brown, beautiful, bold but insipid creature." Many years later it was her son, the Duke of Monmouth, who led the rebellion against James II that ended in the Battle of Sedgmoor.

Lucy Walter was the first. Others followed, at all too frequent intervals, throughout his life. Nell Gwynne, the theater orange-seller, is the best remembered—and best deserves to be, if her warm heart and human kindliness, her wit and her beauty, may be set against her not-so-strict behavior. All too well had Charles learned the lesson of getting on with people, as his mother had wished, but it was always with the other sex that he preferred to exercise his skill.

There was one pleasant and quite innocent little interlude during this period. Jane Lane made her reappearance, for England had become uncomfortable for so royalist a girl. Charles heard she was coming to Paris and rode out to meet her, embraced her warmly, and told everyone how she had saved his life. In his poverty there was little he could do to help her, but he persuaded his sister Mary, who was married to the Prince of Orange, to make her a lady in waiting. Jane went to her new post in Holland, and for years afterwards she and Charles wrote to each other as friends. He never forgot those days when they had ridden pillion as mistress and servant, and when he required an alias as he moved about Europe secretly, it amused him to become "Mr. Jackson" again.

These secret movements were part of what we should call today the "counterrevolution." The most determined royalists were banded together in an underground organization known as the Sealed Knot. They were continually planning armed risings in England. A stream of their agents was forever trickling through the watchful defenses of the Commonwealth. Overseas, the struggle against Cromwell was carried on by every possible means, from the stirring up of resistance in the colonies to the assassination of his ambassadors at foreign courts.

Charles and his supporters could not be expected to see English history as it would be seen by later generations. To them Cromwell was, quite plainly, a traitor, a murderer, and a tyrant. Each new wave of escaping royalists brought fresh news and rumors of the state into which England had fallen. They told of army mutinies and arrests, of closed theaters and disbanded choirs, of deserted racecourses and forbidden amusements. They said less about the other side of the picture—that the roads were now much clearer of highwaymen, that there was more toleration now for the persecuted Quakers, that there were schemes afoot for simplifying the law so the common man could understand it, for treating lunatics more humanely, and for making other reforms.

One thing, above all, provoked the savage amusement of the exiled Cavaliers. Had not the civil war been fought to prove that Parliament was even more sacred than the king? Yet what had Cromwell done at the finish? He had disbanded his precious Parliament, turned them out of doors as his late Majesty would never have dreamed of doing, and set up a military dictatorship in their place! Was not England now parceled out into districts, each ruled by a major general with more absolute power than any king?

Charles and his threadbare court moved like gypsies through a nervous and unfriendly Europe, now at Cologne, now at Bruges, now at Brussels. He was playing tennis in the country not far from this last city when an excited courtier burst in upon the game. The unbelievable had happened. Cromwell, only fifty-eight, with many possible years of vigor before him, had died—supreme irony, on September 3, the anniversary of his victories at Dunbar and Worcester, the day he had himself called "the crowning mercy."

Was this to be a crowning mercy in another sense? Was his death going to crown Charles? After the first delirious rejoicings were over, the exiles had more than a year of weary waiting. Richard Cromwell took his father's place—but only in name, for "Queen Dick" had none of Oliver's personality. Affairs in England drifted into more and more confusion. The thieves were falling out, laughed the exiled Cavaliers; soon the honest men would come into their own. As disunity grew in England, so did the hopes of the Englishmen watching from abroad.

It was a general who settled the question. General Monk, sensing the mood of the nation, marched down from the Scottish border, took control of London, and ordered a general election. It was obvious that the new Parliament would vote to recall Charles to the throne. Without violence, the power slipped from one side to the other. For all the endless debates and documents of those complicated days, the essence of the matter was contained in the song the London apprentices were singing in the streets:

"Ding a ding ding, I heard a bird sing,
The Parliament soldiers are gone to the king!"

And the sailors had gone *for* the King.

Charles had left England in a little brig sailed by two men and a boy: he was brought back from Holland by the whole fleet, sailing across the North Sea, a splendid forest of canvas rippling in the May sunshine. His brothers James and Henry were to go with him. Mary and his Aunt Elizabeth came aboard to kiss him good-by. The flagship, formerly the *Naseby,* was quickly and tactfully renamed the *Royal Charles.* Among the crowd of gentlemen on the deck was a young clerk to the Admiralty, that very Samuel Pepys who, as a schoolboy, had watched the execution of Charles' father, the late King. Charles was scarcely aware of his smiling, overanxious face —there were so many faces that day, all smiling and most of them anxious—but in due time he was to know Mr. Pepys quite well. What he was never to know, and what no man then living was to know, was that Mr. Pepys would record his impressions of that day in a secret diary that no other eye would read until the nineteenth century.

Charles was now within a week of his thirtieth birthday. The sallow, ugly boy had grown into a heavy-featured man who, if not handsome, had a kind of devil-like distinction that appealed more to some people than ordinary good looks. "The Black Boy," some called him. He had the air of a rascal— but at least he was a rascal with an air.

A sardonic smile curved his lips as England battered him with cheers and gun salutes and deafening peals of bells. He had been a fool, he remarked to one companion, not to have come back sooner.

Did not every man he met assure him that he, personally, had been waiting only for this day?

Charles accepted the welcome but he was not fooled by it. Things were not going to be easy. He had one foot in the stirrup of his kingdom: he had yet to show that he could ride the unruly, plunging horse that was the English people.

On one point he was determined: he was not going to lose his head as his father had done, nor was he prepared to "go on his travels again." He was going to be charming to everybody. In some cases the charm came more naturally than others. He quite enjoyed eating the ordinary sailors' breakfast of pork and peas and boiled beef; it took a little more effort to embrace General Monk on Dover beach and call him "father," to pay flattering attentions to Mrs. Monk, and to assure the mayor that he loved the Bible "above all things in the world." But he played his part—tirelessly, one would have said, if there was not evidence how exhausted he was by the end of that first day. It lies in the note he sent to his favorite sister, Minette, before he tumbled wearily into bed at Canterbury:

"My head is so dreadfully stunned with the acclamations of the people, and the vast amount of business, that I know not whether I am writing sense or nonsense."

Every man in the country seemed to be crowding forward to impress his face and name upon the new King. Those who had been abroad for any reason all insisted that they had shared in his exile and, having sacrificed everything in the cause, deserved reward. And those who had stayed behind in England were most anxious to point out that they had done so for the best possible motives. Poor Mr. Pepys was sadly embarrassed, about this time, when he met an old schoolfellow who "did remember that I was a great Roundhead when I was a boy," and there were plenty of public men with much more recent and serious miscalculations that they were anxious to forget.

It was, of course, utterly impossible for Charles to undo the changes of the past eighteen years. He did what he could to reward his loyal supporters, and he was particularly generous to those whose claims he personally knew to be genuine. Once more Jane Lane flits across the stage of history: he gave her a pension and a number of expensive presents. But the whole kingdom could not be turned upside down to put everyone back where he had been in 1642, at the beginning of the civil war.

When it came to punishing the Roundhead leaders, Charles found that the fire of his revenge had burned low. It was not he, but the new Parliament, that insisted on the barbaric digging up and exhibiting of Cromwell's body at Tyburn, and the still more barbaric execution of General Harrison and the other surviving ringleaders in the killing of his father, Charles I. Even so, when less than half the executions had been carried out, he saved the rest of the prisoners by a note to Hyde: "I confess I am weary of hanging—let it sleep." With great difficulty he persuaded his supporters to allow a free pardon to everyone else who had served on the other side.

There had been enough bloodshed.

One of his first moves—it was also partly for economy—was to disband the fine army that Cromwell had created. But some troops he had to have, if only to defend his person against assassins and rioters, so very soon he formed the Life Guards, with the breastplates, scarlet coats, white plumes, and jackboots that have developed into the uniform seen today. A few years later came the Grenadiers. His name is thus associated with the oldest regiments in the British Army; and also (which is in keeping with the warm kindliness of his character) with the well-known Chelsea Hospital for "old soldiers broken in the wars."

Then, as now, the Life Guards stood sentinel at Whitehall. But the Whitehall of Charles II was still the great rambling royal palace where his father had kept court.

The young man who, not so long before, had eaten cheap meals in the taverns of Paris now dined in solitary state in the vast banqueting hall that Inigo Jones had designed under the inspiration of the classical ruins he had seen in Italy. Solitary, because he had as yet no queen to sit beside him; and save when he had royal guests to share his meal, he must eat alone: all the splendid and noble figures crowding the scene were there only to stand and wait or to offer him dishes, humbly kneeling. That was court etiquette, and it had little appeal for Charles. He liked to slip away as soon as the last mouthful was swallowed. He looked forward to the evenings, when he could lay aside this ceremony and relax at private supper parties.

It was easy to be lonely in Whitehall, but difficult to be alone.

If he came in from riding, the long Stone Gallery leading to his apartments was thronged with people hoping to catch his ear for a moment and beg some favor. The place was as public as an art gallery— which was, in fact, just what his picture-collecting father had made of it. For all his warmth and generosity, for all his sympathy with ordinary people, Charles was often compelled to stride through the bowing crowd as fast as he could, ignoring the pathetic eye, the eager smile, and the outstretched paper.

When he had run the gantlet and slipped past the sentries by the velvet-hung doors into the withdrawing room, he could enjoy only what generals call a very "limited withdrawal." Innumerable courtiers had the right to enter there. Many, indeed, had the right to follow him into his bedchamber beyond, a large room overlooking the Thames, where he dealt with State business not handled at his Council table; but here at least, he could exclude others while he held confidential talks with one or two.

For real privacy he must mount a few stairs and unlock the door of the King's Closet. It was the kind of room that today is termed a "den." It was full of clocks and watches, which he loved collecting. They were all ticking away, but they did not always agree, so, distrusting so great a variety of opinions, he used to set his own watch every morning, if the sun shone, by the sundial in the Privy Gardens. Here in the Closet were his other collections—model ships, maps, pictures, jewels, *objets d'art*. Personal friends would be taken in to see these, but only one other man had a key to that locked door—the discreet and faithful Will Chiffinch, officially a "page" of the bedchamber but old enough in years to be Charles' father. Chiffinch knew most, if not all, of Charles' secrets, but no man knew better how to hold his tongue.

One hobby Charles could not practice safely among all these art treasures—and that was chemistry. He had his laboratory immediately below his Closet, so it was perhaps as well that he did not experiment with anything too explosive. He liked to dispense medicines and cordials of his own devising, growing herbs for this purpose in a part of the palace grounds known as the Physic Garden. It was not an unusual interest for a man of his rank and period. Even his adventurous cousin Rupert turned to it in his later years.

Science was in the air. The "Invisible College" founded in his father's time was about to blossom forth, under Charles' encouragement, into the Royal Society we know today. Newton the mathematician, Halley the astronomer, Boyle the chemist, and Wren the many-sided genius who finally concentrated on architecture—these were only four outstanding figures among the many alert and able men who made this the first great period of scientific progress in England.

Charles himself, of course, had neither the time nor the intellect to follow them into the higher realms of speculation. Apart from State business, too many other interests called him. Few men lived more fully.

Puritans—and even less strait-laced persons— might shake their heads over his late nights and candlelit supper parties. Nonetheless, the King was often up and playing tennis by six o'clock in the morning, or galloping along the road to Hampton Court at five. With his brother James he would go swimming in the Thames at Putney or Battersea (Henry, alas, died of smallpox a few months after the three royal brothers regained their childhood home), and he was never happier than when he was afloat, sailing a new type of craft called a "yacht" presented to him by the Dutch government, or the improved version of it that was quickly designed by the famous English shipbuilder, Peter Pett. Other days found him riding after the stag or running with old Chiffinch's beagles. He was nearly forty-five when, after three keenly contested heats, he rode the winner himself in the Newmarket Plate. No man as fit as Charles could be accused of ruining his health by late hours and riotous living.

He loved fresh air, whether it carried the scent of grass and flowers or the salty tang of the sea. London smoke, already a nuisance, he hated. Sportsman though he was, he liked gentler exercise as well, strolling in park and garden with people to talk to and his dogs rollicking at his heels. It is to Charles that Londoners owe the artificial lake in St. James's Park and the oldest of the trees that grow there. He was the first to stock the park with birds, and went to feed the ducks like any modern visitor. But he maintained a miniature zoo there, as well, with antelope and deer and other animals.

Indoors, he liked good talk, dancing, gay music, and the theater. The stately masques continued, as in his mother's and his grandmother's day, but Charles preferred the public playhouses in Drury Lane and Lincoln's Inn Fields. Here, after the long Puritan ban, the English drama was born anew and utterly different. Gone were the last lovely fancies of the Shakespearean age. Prose took the place of poetry, just as bold-eyed actresses took over the female parts once played only by boys. Cynical, coarse wit and worldly wisdom took the place of romance. It was the mood of the court. Only a few older people sighed for the old-fashioned plays of their youth. Was one, perhaps, his own aunt Elizabeth, who remembered the first production of a comedy called *The Tempest* and being told that the girl heroine, Miranda, was intended for herself? Yet the Restoration drama, though little more than tarnished silver beside the pure gold of the best earlier plays, made its own contribution to the total wealth of English literature.

Such, then, was the day-to-day life of the King.

It did not alter much after he married.

A king in those days could not expect to marry for love. He must wed some foreign princess, whom perhaps he had never seen, so that their two countries could benefit from the alliance. The best he could hope for was to fall in love with her later. That happened quite often. It had happened to the first Charles.

After just two years of bachelor kingship, Charles chose a Portuguese princess, Catherine of Braganza, as his bride. She was a dark, dainty, rather solemn little thing. Her teeth were a bit prominent, but she had beautiful hands, and in her rose-colored wedding dress, with her dark eyes liquid and bright with the excitement of it all, she was not unattractive. She brought with her as dowry the port of Tangier in Morocco, opposite Gibraltar, and the Portuguese settlement at Bombay, which was to prove most valuable to British trade with India.

Charles rode to meet her at Portsmouth, where she had just landed, still queasy after the voyage from Lisbon. The next morning they were married secretly, to please her, by a Roman Catholic priest, and after dinner publicly, to please the nation, by a bishop of the Church of England. A few days later they set out for Hampton Court for their honeymoon. May was just turning into June, the weather was kind, and the place was looking its best. They were able to have picnics and to go boating. Coming from Portugal, Catherine was delighted by the freshness of the early summer flowers and the sheer greenness of English lawns and leaves.

She fell in love with Charles. For him, the miracle

never happened. He could never surrender his heart to her as he could to others. He treated her with a strange mixture of kindness and cruelty, at times going to great lengths of tenderness and considera-tion, at others almost breaking her heart by his thoughtless and unfeeling behavior. Catherine took him as she found him: wayward, faithless, yet some-how at the end always forgivable. She put up with everything and gave him a lifelong affection in re-turn.

Matters might have gone differently if they had had children. As it was, most of the reign was clouded by the background problem of the succes-sion. If Charles died without an heir, the crown would pass to his brother. James was a stanch Ro-man Catholic and would never, like Charles, play the hypocrite in religion to please the people. All that Parliament could do was insist that James's little daughters, Mary and Anne, should be brought up in the Church of England. Charles often warned his brother that unless he learned to handle the English more skillfully, he would lose his head or at least his crown, and it took the obstinate James only four years as king to prove Charles right.

Charles himself was a past master in handling his turbulent subjects. He had his own strong views, but he always knew when to give way gracefully if it was unavoidable.

For the first seven years, while he was settling himself in the saddle, he let Hyde run things pretty much his own way. But he had no real use for Hyde's theory of a partnership between king and Parliament; when Hyde grew old, pompous, and dogmatic, and had made himself unpopular with everyone, Charles took the reins in his own hands.

In his heart he wanted to be a despot (though a benevolent one) like his cousin King Louis XIV, across the Channel. Charles loved everything French. It was, after all, his mother's country and now the home of Minette, who was married to the French king's brother. It was the country where, despite shortage of cash, he had spent some merry times as a young exile. It was the land of good breeding and polished manners, of civilization and elegance. Charles made his court as French as he dared. He found that the upper classes in England (despite the grumblings of the mob) would take a great deal from France—etiquette, standards of taste, music, and a new sparkling wine called champagne. Would they, he wondered, take the French system of an absolute king?

It might be done, he reckoned, if Louis backed him and gave him enough money, from the deep coffers of France, to govern England without needing to call Parliament.

With his sister's help he planned the secret Treaty of Dover. When he judged the moment right, he was to announce himself a Roman Catholic. When Louis gave the word, England was to attack France's enemy, Holland. In return, Louis was to keep him well supplied with gold.

Minette obtained her husband's permission to visit Charles for a few days at Dover while these points were being settled. Brother and sister enjoyed one of the happiest weeks of their lives, for the secret conferences were well varied with court festivities of every sort. When, reluctantly, she had to go home, Charles sailed halfway across the Channel to snatch another hour or two of her company.

They never met again. Within the month Minette was dead, after a sudden attack of peritonitis. "I have loved Charles better than life itself," she murmured as her eyes closed. "My only regret in dying is to be leaving him."

"My grief for her is so great," said Charles a short while afterwards, "that I dare not allow myself to dwell upon it. I try so far as possible to think of other things."

Her death did not, of course, affect the treaty Charles had signed, unknown to anyone in England except a handful of his ministers. After waiting a year or two, he put the plan into action by coming out as Louis' ally against Holland and by announcing religious freedom at home, as a prelude to his own change of church. But at once the horse reared under him: the English people would not have such a policy. With a violent effort he regained his seat in the saddle, canceled his measure concerning religion, broke his alliance, and made a separate peace with the Dutch.

He did not make the same mistake again. After that he got his own way as far as he could by subtle, indirect methods—rigging the Parliamentary elections so as to obtain a majority of his own supporters, and letting ministers take the blame for whatever proved unpopular. "The king can do no wrong." The tradition suited Charles well enough. Some wit hung a paper on the door of the bed-chamber:

> *"Here lies our Sovereign Lord the King,*
> *Whose word no man relies on.*
> *He never said a foolish thing,*
> *And never did a wise one."*

Charles took the joke with his usual urbane good-humor. "Quite true," he remarked, "for my words are my own—but my acts are my ministers' !"

Politically minded men might attack his policies. They might elect—in spite of all his tricks—a majority of Whigs, the opposition party with this strange new Scottish name signifying "spurrers on"; and such a Parliamentary majority might force him to do this or that. But the people at large would never rise against this sportsman king who supped with the jockeys at Newmarket and was hail-fellow-well-met with every class of society. They remembered how he had stood amid the blazing ruins of London in the Great Fire of 1666, passing buckets with his own hands and scattering golden guineas to the demolition gangs. They remembered how he had taken command of his troops when the Dutch fleet had sailed up the Thames and threatened the city. They remembered how, when the mutinous sailors rioted in the Strand, he had ridden into their midst and so pacified them that they gave him three lusty cheers before they dispersed. Yes, King Charles was all right. . . .

He kept them in that frame of mind for a quarter of a century, and could have done so longer. But in February, 1685, the end came suddenly. Charles had a seizure as he was getting up one morning. For several days he lingered between life and death, suffering agonies—even more from his doctors than from his disease—yet never losing the courage, the humor, and the thoughtfulness for others that had always marked him. He apologized to his lords for being so long a-dying. More seriously, he begged the Queen's pardon for all his shortcomings. On the last evening a Roman Catholic priest was smuggled into his room in disguise, and Charles was received into the Church that was his mother's, his brother's, and his wife's.

Toward dawn he murmured: "Open the curtains that I may once more see day." They did so. Gradually the winter light grew stronger. He was never to see it fade. Just before twelve he slipped out of the world he had loved so ardently, and James II was King.

The faithful, wicked old Chiffinch was with his master to the end. He was still Page of the Backstairs, at the ripe age of eighty-two, still friend and keeper of the King's secrets. But the secrets of death were something he could not share for a few years longer. Charles had passed through a private door, of which even Will Chiffinch was as yet denied the key.

† † † † † †

WILLIAM III: THE

DUTCH GENERAL

"About ten at night the Prince came home, and he found an easy admission. His attendance very inconsiderable as for a Prince; but yet handsome, and his tutor a fine man, and himself a very pretty boy."

So wrote Mr. Pepys in his diary at the Hague, in May, 1660. On the following day he was to see and kiss the hand of his new sovereign, Charles II. But amid all the excitements of the Restoration it could scarcely have entered his head that within those few hours he had seen two other future kings of England—not only Charles' younger brother James, but his nine-year-old nephew, then Prince of Orange but one day to be King William III.

Pepys was right in noting that his "attendance" was "very inconsiderable." Despite his princely rank and ancient family, the boy counted for little in Holland. The country was a prosperous middle-class republic. There was no court, no aristocracy to speak of. Nothing to compare with the stately splendor Englishmen remembered from the days of Charles I, and most certainly nothing to hold a candle to the dazzling glories of the Sun King, Louis XIV, at Fontainebleau.

"The Hague is a most neat place in all respects," wrote Pepys. "The houses so neat in all places and things as is possible." Not very descriptive—yet in that one word "neat" he had struck the keynote. The whole country was as neat and regular as one of its own tulip fields. Efficiency, cleanliness, progress, invention—those were the qualities in which Holland was leading Europe at that time. The very land had a geometrical straightness: without those long horizontals of embankment and canal, much of Holland would have been lost beneath the untidy sea.

Pepys was not perhaps quite so accurate when he described William as "a very pretty boy." True, the young prince had inherited some of the Stuart features from his mother—the dark almond eyes, the reddish-brown hair, the full mouth in the oval face—but he had been delicate from birth and was never exactly glowing with health. Time was to tighten those full lips and narrow those dark eyes, until sometimes they would close completely for an instant, at the pressure of the aching cares in the brain behind them. Smallpox would come and mark a skin toughened by wind and rain and the smoke of many battles. These changes were to come later, but even at nine William was by no means the ideal healthy, carefree small boy. Pepys, however, was too much of a snob to admit, even in his most private diary, that one of princely rank could be anything but "very pretty."

William had never known his father, who had died of smallpox eight days before the boy was born. William had therefore been brought up mainly by his mother, who had supervised his early lessons just as her own had been supervised by her conscientious father, Charles I. As Mary had been an English princess, William might very well have grown up with more knowledge of England, and affection for English ways, than he actually did. But it must be remembered that Mary's mother had been French and her father had been the child of Scottish and Danish parents, so she had no strictly English blood or at least only a few drops, much diluted down the years. Also, it was a long time since she had lived in England. She had been married in 1641, before the civil war, though it was not until nine years later, on November 4, 1650, that William was born. Until the day in 1660 when Pepys came over with the fleet to fetch back her brother to his throne, England had been no place for members of the Stuart family to visit.

She saw that her little son was taught English, along with French and German, and he was an obedient pupil, though his English was never perfect and he could never get rid of his Dutch accent. He learned mathematics, too, and "military science," though it is a little difficult to imagine how much of the latter subject he could have understood during his mother's lifetime. For, a few months after the Restoration, when she was in England visiting Charles and sharing in the celebrations of his homecoming, she caught smallpox and died, as her husband had done.

An orphan at ten, William faced the world alone. Nor was it a very friendly world.

From his earliest years William had been taught about the special and peculiar position his family occupied.

He knew that his title came from nowhere in Holland but from a tiny pocket of independent territory in southern France. Orange was an ancient Roman town, with ruins of a magnificent theater and triumphal arch, near the Rhone River. William never saw the place, and its classical remains would scarcely have appealed to his severely practical mind. Orange lay deep in France, which, throughout his life, was hostile territory, even during those years when there was no open war in progress.

The title had come into William's family, the Nassaus, more than a hundred years before. Much more important to them, though, was another title —that of Stadtholder, or chief magistrate in the Dutch republic, which had been voted to them forever.

The Dutch republic had come into existence, in the previous century, when the people drove out their Spanish masters. Among William's earliest impressions were the faded Spanish standards— trophies of victory and national liberation—that hung in the great hall of his palace at the Hague.

That palace, like the post of Stadtholder, had been given to his family for their outstanding leadership in bygone days. William might be proud to know that his ancestors included the ancient kings of England and Scotland; he was probably even more proud that, on his father's side, he was the descendant of Holland's hero, William the Silent.

Bygone glories were all very well, but the orphaned boy, pacing sadly through the lonely galleries of his moated palace, or riding, without brothers or sisters or close friends, through the oak woods outside the town, must have wondered how he would ever be able to live up to them.

His mother, on dying, had appointed her brother, King Charles of England, as his guardian. But Charles, far away in London, had other matters to think about. William was left to grow up as best he could at the Hague, the Dutch government paying the expenses of his household but not showing any great interest in his future—if indeed he had one.

The Dutch (the boy realized, as he grew older) saw no further need for the House of Orange that had led them to independence. Strictly, the country was a republic, known as the United Netherlands to distinguish it from the Spanish Netherlands, which are now Belgium and Luxembourg. The republic was governed by a body known as the States General, representing the various provinces, of which "North Holland" and "South Holland" were only two. There was no reason why the "presidency," or office of Stadtholder, should be reserved for the Princes of Orange. Oliver Cromwell, indeed, had bullied the Dutch into voting that it should *not* be. If Charles II did nothing else for his nephew, he at least had got them to alter that and to give back to William the office held by his forefathers.

In certain ways—not only their republican form of government but their practical outlook and their tremendous enterprise—the Dutch in that century had a good deal in common with the Americans of today.

William realized that the heart of Holland beat not in the quiet Hague (except for a few days now and then when the States General met in solemn assembly) but in the bustling Exchange of Amsterdam, thirty miles to the north. Like Venice, Amsterdam was a city built on piles amid the swamps, but whereas Venice was a trading port in decline, Amsterdam was the biggest and wealthiest city in Europe.

Holland might be small, no more than half the area of Wales, but she was immensely wealthy. The Bank of Amsterdam was the financial center of Europe, as the Bank of England was to be later— indeed, the Bank of England was founded in William's reign, wth help from the Dutch institution.

William never forgot he was a prince. His own interests and enthusiasms were princely: he was a horseman and a hunting man, a soldier and a statesman. He had his own opinions about the hardheaded bankers and merchants who ran the affairs of his country while he was a boy; but as a Dutchman he could hardly fail to be proud of that country's position in the world.

He saw the Dutch East India Company's fleets sailing to the ends of the world and bringing back fabulous cargoes. He knew that Dutch shipbuilders had no superiors in Europe. Dutch cattle were the best. Dutch farmers led the way in everything. They were the first to grow fields of turnips, potatoes, clover, and other crops for winter feed; they were already famous for their dairy produce, even before there was the quick modern transport needed for an export trade. It was the same with market gardening and ornamental gardening; the Dutch tulip was already famous wherever men talked of flowers. Holland was celebrated for her fabrics and her porcelain, her metalwork and her diamond cutting, and a variety of other skills.

And though her citizens might be businessmen, they were not indifferent to culture. Some Dutch portrait painters might cross the North Sea to seek their fortune at the English court, but most artists found plenty of commissions at home. The University of Leyden was rated higher among scholars than either Oxford or Cambridge, and it was said that more books were published in Holland than in the rest of Europe put together. Certainly both Dutch printing and engraving were advanced far beyond English standards.

William had no cause to feel inferior because he had been born in the small country of Holland.

What was more to the point was the question:

how could he restore his family's position in a republic that felt no need of him?

Another blow fell upon him in the year of his mother's death. King Louis decided to mop up the patch of independent territory in the midst of his kingdom. His troops invaded Orange and dismantled the fortifications. Now, more than ever, William's title "Prince of Orange" had an empty sound.

The real power in Holland, all this time, was the Pensionary, or chief minister, Jan De Witt. His supporters called him "the Wisdom of Holland." There was a feud between the De Witt family and the House of Orange—Jan's father had been imprisoned by William's—and so long as Jan and his brother Cornelius controlled affairs, the boy knew that nothing would be done to restore his fortunes.

It was De Witt who had the last word in his upbringing, until he was of full age. William learned to keep his thoughts to himself. He had little interest in sports and games—riding and hunting were the only kinds of exercise he enjoyed—and there were few chances of friendship with other boys, though there was one, Jan Willem van Bentinck, two years older than he, who remained his trusted companion for the rest of his life. Otherwise, William was very much of a lone wolf. Like William I, six hundred years earlier, he had been born to a troubled inheritance. He had to learn the lessons of patience and craftiness so as to survive the dangers around him. The first essential was to reach manhood. When he was a man and no longer a boy, he would know how to strike, and where.

He was nearly fifteen when war broke out with England. An English fleet took possession of the Dutch colony on Manhattan Island, and its name was changed from "New Amsterdam" to "New York" in honor of the sea-loving duke, William's Uncle James. The war was a naval one, wasteful to both sides, and the honors were about even. Peace was made after a couple of years, and the English ambassador, Sir William Temple, came over with a grand scheme for a Triple Alliance between England, Holland, and Sweden, the three great Protestant nations of northern Europe.

What a mistake, argued Temple, for such natural allies to fall out among themselves! They should unite against the real enemy, France, which, under the ambitious Louis, was seeking to dominate Europe.

Temple's suggestion appealed especially to the Dutch. They were by far the easiest mouthful for Louis to gobble up, for they alone had no sea between themselves and France, and all their warships were of no avail against the swarming masses of the French Army. De Witt welcomed the new alliance, and William, who differed on so many other points, entirely agreed on this one. A united front against France was the object he worked for throughout his career.

Temple was to have a big influence on William's life—but not yet. De Witt, as Pensionary, was the man who mattered and the man he had to deal with. The Prince of Orange was a powerless boy, still in his teens.

After the war with England was over, De Witt resumed his vendetta against the last survivor of the House of Orange.

An edict was passed abolishing the office of Stadtholder. De Witt called upon William and told him he must leave the palace.

William retorted that it was his family home and had been for generations.

True, admitted the Pensionary. But legally the palace was public property. As a matter of courtesy the Princes of Orange had been allowed to live in it, but now . . .

William considered. He had seen this struggle coming. Had the time come to make a stand? Was he old enough now to assert himself? If he let himself be turned out, would he ever regain his position? He knew the strength of De Witt and his supporters. How strong was the sentiment of the people for their princely house?

Long odds did not frighten him. He made his decision. If the States General wanted him out of his home, they would have to turn him out by force.

De Witt eyed the sullen, determined boy and bit his lip. It was his turn now to take stock of the situation. Much as he wanted revenge for the humiliation his own father had suffered in days gone by, he saw that if he pressed this point he might overreach himself.

In the end, rather than risk a popular outcry in sympathy with the prince, De Witt and his supporters dropped the idea. William stayed on in the moated palace where the tattered Spanish banners drooped from the walls. He had won his own first little victory. And now he must not stand on the defensive, he must press his advantage. He was eighteen. Old enough, and ready, to fight.

Sir William Temple has left us a description of William as he now appeared: "A young man of more parts than ordinary, and of the better sort; that is, not lying in that kind of wit which is neither of use to oneself nor to anybody else, but in good plain sense which showed application if he had business that deserved it; and this with extreme good and agreeable humor and dispositions without any vice; that he was asleep in bed always at ten o'clock; loved hunting as much as he hated swearing, and preferred cock-ale before any wine."

William, in short, was just the type of young man that any worthy, God-fearing merchant in Holland would have welcomed as a son-in-law. His religious views, his habits, his tastes had nothing in common with those overgay Stuarts across the water in wicked London. In all that was known about him there was no cause for alarm.

His first move was to appear before the public assembly of Zealand, the province at the extreme southwestern edge of the country. Politely he reminded them that he had reached the age at which, in the past, they had always elected his forefathers "first noble" of the province. The Zealanders exchanged glances, debated, and then decided to maintain the family tradition. William had privately hoped that they might go further and choose him as their own Stadtholder, but they did not. Still, he had made a beginning. The position of "first noble" entitled him to a seat in the States General as representative of the Zealand nobility, such as it was.

Two years later, in his twentieth year, William paid his first visit to England. It was no difficult journey in time of peace—London and the Hague were closer, in traveling time, than London and York or London and Exeter. London was full of Dutch businessmen, clustered around their own church at Austin Friars; and there were Dutchmen scattered in outlying counties such as Devon and Cambridgeshire, where the engineer Vermuyden had a Dutch-style house with the motto carved in stone over the door, *Niet Zonder Arbeit,* "not without labor."

William would have had little sensation of being a stranger in a strange land, if his visit had been spent in these circles. But in England he was very much the Prince of Orange and a Stuart. London gave him a civic banquet, Oxford gave him an honorary degree, but for the rest of the time he was mainly at Whitehall, breathing what he felt to be the tainted air of his uncle's scandalous court. He viewed his uncles with suspicion. James, of course, was an open Roman Catholic. Charles he was not sure of—but if that cynical, worldly monarch had any religious leanings at all, William would have guessed that they tilted the same way. He was overfond of the French, too. . . . How far, the prince wondered, could he be trusted to support this Triple Alliance against

Louis, for which Sir William Temple, his own ambassador, had worked so hard?

During this visit William met his cousin—"she-cousin," as Pepys would have termed her—the eight-year-old Mary, James' elder daughter. A pretty, sweet-natured child, she was not often to be seen at court, which was just as well, William grimly concluded, at her tender age. She lived at Richmond Palace mostly, in the care of Lady Frances Villiers, who had a tribe of children of her own. William was glad to find that her father had not been allowed to influence her toward his own views: Parliament insisted that Mary, as a possible heiress to the throne, must be brought up as a member of the Church of England. Her chances of ever wearing the crown might not be very great—the Queen might yet have a child, or James' new second wife from Italy might have a baby boy to displace his half sisters in the order of succession—but in such troubled times every possibility had to be considered. With Europe divided into two camps by religion, the faith held by the ruler of England was no private matter but a life-and-death political question to millions of people.

So, noting his uncles' inclinations—the one open, the other masked and doubtful—William looked with hope and interest at his little cousin. Perhaps some day, if all went well, they would be allies in the cause, she Queen of England and he Stadtholder of the United Provinces. It is most unlikely that another possibility ever entered his mind at this stage, that one day they would be also husband and wife.

That was 1670. William returned home, and in little more than a year his worst suspicions about his Uncle Charles were confirmed.

In 1671 Charles met Minette, as related in the previous chapter, and signed the secret Treaty of Dover with the French king. Though William knew nothing of this at the time, his shrewd eye began to note signs of the approaching storm. The English ambassador was recalled—that good friend of Holland, Sir William Temple, who had dryly summed up King Louis as "a great comet, expecting not only to be gazed at but admired." And Temple had been so disgusted by whatever he had found out on his return to London that he had resigned and retired into private life. Evidently something was brewing that Temple disagreed with—and that something was unlikely to be to Holland's advantage. In Sweden, too, where an inefficient council of regents was governing the country for the boy king, Karl XI, the French were using bribes to break up the northern alliance.

De Witt had been much slower than William to see these danger signals. He had trusted not only Charles (which was understandable) but Louis also, though he was the obvious enemy. Louis had flattered him, agreed with him about the House of Orange, and congratulated him on keeping the young prince out of power. De Witt had many good qualities, but when the Orange family was mentioned, he lost all sense of balance. To him, the young prince at the Hague must always be the real enemy, not any king in Paris or London.

But at last even De Witt saw the storm that was about to burst. He asked Louis the meaning of various warlike preparations, and he was told blandly that he would know in the spring.

Obviously, war with France was coming. And only if Dutchmen of all parties closed their ranks could the enemy be beaten back. William the Silent could have led them to victory. Could his great-grandson do so now?

William, now just twenty-one, found himself appointed Captain General of the Dutch forces. De Witt had yielded reluctantly to popular demand. There was not a day to lose. William began to examine the resources at his disposal, and as he did so his face took on an even grimmer look than usual. The De Witt government had shockingly neglected the defenses. Veteran troops had been disbanded, important commands had been put in the hands of mere civilians, officers had grown slack in their duties.

William himself had had no firsthand experience of war, but all his young life he had been keenly interested in strategy and fortification. He had toughened his own weak body by riding and hunting, which he thought of as training for cavalry warfare. With sufficient time and a free hand, he knew he could reorganize the army—but he had neither. De Witt had managed to hamper him by getting all sorts of petty conditions and restrictions attached to his appointment, and he was only to hold it for a year.

In his blacker moods William may have wondered whether he had been right to accept it at all. Was it a trap, a trick of De Witt's to discredit him with the Dutch people? Suppose Holland could not stave off the French attack. Who would be blamed for her surrender—William, the general commanding her armies, or De Witt, the minister who had previously neglected them? Was De Witt more anxious to defeat the King of France—or the Prince of Orange?

In the spring of 1672 the storm burst. England declared war on Holland, and France sent her armies swarming over the Dutch frontier as remorselessly as a flood tide from the North Sea. The defenses went down like sand castles. Large garrisons hauled down their flags without firing a shot. De Witt, seized with panic, proposed surrender.

Then occurred one of those extraordinary national upheavals that sometimes convulse a people in the hour of disaster, when the man in the street is braver, in his ignorance of the odds, than the government sitting in council with the hopeless facts before them. And when, in the end, the ignorant man in the street is proved to be right.

All eyes turned to the Prince of Orange. At Dordrecht, the historic town where the Dutch had held their first assembly after driving out the Spaniards just one hundred years before, there was a great demonstration in favor of William. The magistrates met and revoked their previous edict that had ended his position as Stadtholder. The news was carried from city to city. Hurried meetings were called. In one place after another, William was voted back into his family's traditional office. The States General came together and solemnly confirmed the people's verdict. De Witt and his brother Cornelius were denounced as traitors. They were saved once from assassination, but soon afterwards the mob raided their prison and savagely lynched them in the street. William shed no tears over his dead enemies; he had other matters to occupy him.

Holland had risen as one man to repel the invader and wipe out the disgrace of those first surrenders. As one man? Even the women and children flung themselves into the struggle. In front of Ardenburg they joined with their menfolk—a mere two hundred citizens and a hundred soldiers—and held back a French force estimated at five thousand. At Groningen the university students manned the defenses along with the townsmen and boasted that they had withstood thirty thousand besiegers. Some reports might be exaggerated, but of one thing there was no doubt: William's leadership had stirred up a new spirit in Holland.

Was spirit enough, he wondered, against the sheer weight of the invading hordes? Louis had sent a hundred and twenty thousand men into Holland. The Dutch, unsurpassed at sea, could not possibly muster enough land forces to hold them. The French were what the Spaniards had been a century before, the finest soldiers in Europe. But whereas Spain had been far away and reinforcement difficult, France was near and therefore more dangerous. Would captured French banners ever hang beside the faded Spanish trophies at the Hague?

The French banners nearly did reach the Hague —but if they had done so, they would have flown over the palace in triumph, not drooped indoors. The Dutch had resorted to their traditional method of defense: they had breached the dykes and let the sea flood great stretches of the country. This held up the enemy during that first season of the war, but when winter returned and the water froze, they were able to advance across the ice. They would have reached the Hague if there had not been a sudden thaw.

Still, the war had not proved as simple as Louis had expected. He and Charles offered terms. Charles, in particular, had only good will for his nephew personally: it was De Witt whom Charles had disliked, and with De Witt gone and William in power, he would have been only too glad to get out of a war that his own subjects hated. He suggested that William become the sovereign ruler of Holland, protected and guaranteed by Louis and himself.

William rejected the offer scornfully. He would rule Holland as the elected Stadtholder of the Dutch people, but he had no desire to be forced upon them by their foreign enemies.

"I will never betray the trust of my country that my ancestors have so long defended," he declared. If need be, he would "die in the last dyke." He urged the States General to continue the war. Even if the country were overrun, they should take ship and maintain the struggle from their East Indian colonies. So, in 1672, William set the example that was to be followed by the Dutch Government after the German invasion of 1940.

It did not come to that, for William. He held on to a good deal of territory, fighting the French with dogged determination while, at sea, his admiral De Ruyter gave the English fleet rather more punishment than he received. Meanwhile, William was learning to be a general. He took several towns and failed to take others. He was sound rather than brilliant, but his men were quick to note that he took care of them and threw no lives away uselessly. If he had to retreat, he had the knack of doing so with the minimum of loss to his own army and the maximum to its pursuers.

Only with his own life was he ever careless. In the third summer of the war he fought a day-long battle at Seneff against the famous French commander, the Prince of Condé. The casualties were heavy on both sides, but the result doubtful. Condé remarked afterwards, admiringly, that William had behaved throughout the day like a veteran general except in one single respect: he always exposed himself to fire like a rash recruit.

There was no doubt that William loved soldiering. He was never so happy as when he was living the hard life of the camp.

The year after Seneff he caught smallpox, the curse of his age and of his own family in particular.

For a few days his followers held their breath. William was now the one hope of their country. They had made him Stadtholder for life, they had voted the office perpetually to his sons and grandsons after him. Was he to die now, as both his parents had died before him—but, unlike them, unmarried and leaving no heir to carry on the House of Orange?

William recovered. The war went on. Gradually, for all the heroic resistance of the Dutch, the superior weight of the French was beginning to tell. William realized that it was not enough to be a general, he must be a statesman, too. He could never hope to beat France. Sooner or later he would have to make terms, and rather worse terms than he had wished for. His duty to Holland was to get the best terms he could.

First he would go for the weak point in the alliance against him. The English people were half-hearted about a war they had never wanted, and they had forced Charles to make a separate peace with him after two years. Now was the time to bring Holland and England back into their old friendship and link them in a way that no secret plottings between Charles and Louis could break.

William decided to marry his cousin Mary, who was now fifteen.

Choosing a good moment, when both Charles and his chief minister Danby were in difficulties, he arranged a state visit to London. Charles was obviously anxious to see the long-drawn-out war between France and Holland brought to some conclusion. He wanted William to accept reasonable terms and was quite willing to offer his niece in marriage as an inducement. William was a firm bargainer, however. Marriage first, he insisted. Then he would discuss the peace. If anyone was to trust another, he preferred that Charles should trust him rather than the other way around.

Charles shrugged his shoulders and agreed; James (the girl's father) flew into a passion but obeyed the King; Mary* dissolved into floods of tears; and Louis, when he heard the news, took it "like the loss of an army." The calmest actor in all this drama was almost certainly the bridegroom himself.

There was one more summer of fighting after that. On August 11, 1678, the States General accepted (while William was absent at the front) a peace with France on worse terms than he had confidently expected to get after his visit to England. Three days later—before official dispatches had reached him from the Hague—he won a major victory over the French at Mons.

It was too late to make any difference. Messengers arrived while the dead were still being buried. The war was over.

William was now a man in his late twenties, a man's man with gruff ways and no graces, serious, careworn, old beyond his years.

Mary was in her middle teens, young even for her

* The story of this wedding is told more fully in *The Seven Queens of England*.

age and unsophisticated, frivolous in her tastes—dancing and acting and card playing, even on Sundays—yet, with it all, surprisingly innocent and unspoiled by the English court life from which she had been so suddenly snatched.

They were an ill-assorted couple. But the marriage, which had begun so unromantically, turned out surprisingly well.

Mary fell in love with this dour, tight-lipped, stocky soldier, whom another Englishwoman, Celia Fiennes, was soon to describe in her journal as "our Hero King William the Third tho' little in stature yet great in achievements and valour." She fell in love, too, with Holland and the new home that he had prepared for her, the lovely Palace in the Wood, surrounded by the oak forests outside the Hague.

Mary was essentially a home-loving person, and that was just what William needed. He did not want a politically-minded wife who would expect to discuss every problem with him. When he came home from council chamber or military camp, he preferred to relax.

An orphan since his tenth year, he had known little home life, and Mary gave him a quiet happiness he had never before enjoyed. He was not good at showing his feelings—years of hiding them from De Witt and other enemies had made him reserved, and he was too old now to alter his ways. But though he could not match Mary's openhearted devotion to himself, he developed a deep affection for her that grew stronger every year.

The marriage had been made for political reasons, and though it became more and more a genuine human marriage of two people, it did not lose its political importance.

There was peace now with France, but William had no illusions. Someday the unfinished struggle with Louis would be resumed. Meanwhile, he must gather the allies he had lacked before: Sweden, the German princes, even the Catholic emperor in Spain. Anyone, in fact, who would resist Louis' ambition to be master of Europe. England was vital to William's plan of defense, but England, under Charles II, was always the doubtful factor.

She became even more doubtful when Charles died and James II succeeded him. Though James had become (most reluctantly) William's father-in-law eight years earlier, all his sympathies were with Catholic France.

William began to watch affairs in England very carefully. His wife was heiress to the throne. Her younger sister Anne came next, and he himself was third in line, as a grandson of Charles I. He was not interested in England for its own sake but only as an essential piece in the jigsaw puzzle of defense against Louis. The completion of that jigsaw was the work fate had given him, and all his life was directed to it.

Two years after James's accession, he sent over a trusted emissary, Dykevelt, to spy out the land, make contacts with English statesmen, and to remind them that, in case of need, the rightful heiress to the crown was the Princess of Orange, just across the North Sea.

James was already showing, by his tactless and dictatorial behavior, how shrewd his brother had been in prophesying that he could easily lose his throne. It took James barely two years more to prove Charles completely right.

In the spring of 1688 William received a visitor at the Hague. He was Edward Russell, nephew of the Earl of Bedford. He brought a long tale of complaint about the King's actions in trying to force his own religion upon the country.

Russell ended by urging William to invade England with an army, in defense of "the laws of England and the Protestant religion."

William, wary as ever, would not promise anything. He could only do so, he said, if invited by the principal men in the kingdom. At the back of his mind, too, was the knowledge that if he left Holland with any large force, Louis might seize the chance to declare war. However critical the situation in England, he must not leave his own country undefended.

That summer events moved swiftly.

First came the famous trial of the seven bishops who had made a stand against James. They were acquitted amid wild scenes of rejoicing. Within a day or two William held in his hands the invitation he had asked for—signed in code by Lord Shrewsbury, Lord Devonshire, the Bishop of London, and other key men in the opposition to James.

After another week came very different news from England. After years of childless marriage, a baby son had been born to James and his second wife. William's face darkened. This baby altered the whole line of succession. Mary, Anne, himself, they were all three out of the running. . . . James, one could depend upon it, would have this child brought up with his own ideas, not those of Parliament.

If William was ever for a moment insincere in his religious observances, it was surely at that moment when he knelt in his private chapel at the Hague and muttered "Amen" to the new prayer added to the service on behalf of the royal baby. There was an added bitterness in the thought that he and Mary had been childless all these years and there was no heir to the House of Orange.

More news came winging its way across the North Sea. Astounding rumors were circulating in London: that the newborn infant was not the child of the King and Queen at all, but one that had been smuggled into the palace in a warming pan . . . that an elaborate plot had been made to cheat the English people by introducing a false prince, since no real one existed, so that Mary could be robbed of her rights to the throne.

William's brow puckered as he read dispatch after dispatch from his friends and agents across the water. Everyone there seemed to be convinced that the rumors were true. Even Princess Anne had reluctantly come to the conclusion that her father and stepmother had joined in a plot against her sister and herself. All kinds of circumstances were highly suspicious. It was altogether too lucky a coincidence for the King that after all these years he should suddenly be blessed with a son and heir when he most needed one.

Nowadays most people believe the baby was really the child of the King and Queen, and the warming-pan story is dismissed as propaganda. But it was widely accepted at the time, and William and Mary—with only their friends in England to guide them—had a good excuse to accept it. Did William truly in his heart believe it? That is something we shall never know. A man believes what he wants to believe. And if historians today still cannot feel absolutely positive of the facts in this case, William was certainly in no position to be certain at the time.

He had come to a turning point in his life. If he did nothing now, made no sign, it would mean that he acknowledged the child as the next King of England. It meant a breach in the defense system against France that would never be filled in his own lifetime.

William began to muster ships and troops. Louis warned James, offered French forces, suggested that Portsmouth should become a French base in England. James, pigheaded and blind to his danger, was only aware that such French interference would stir his unruly subjects still more hotly against him. He refused the offer. Louis shrugged his shoulders and, having schemes of his own afoot, sent his armies off to invade Germany. That was the best news William had heard for a long time. It was safe to leave Holland now; the way to England was clear.

In October he issued a manifesto listing the various ways in which King James was flouting the laws of England. The sole object of his own journey was to ensure the calling of a free Parliament (just as General Monk had done before Charles II's restoration), so that a proper inquiry could be made into the true identity of the alleged prince. Once this was done, he would immediately withdraw his troops.

Six days after this manifesto, William made a farewell speech to the States General. He was not an emotional orator, but he deeply stirred his listeners. If there was a dry eye in the assembly, it was his own.

Two days later the States General voted to support his expedition. It was not, of course, a purely Dutch venture. There were a good number of English exiles, ranging from William's political adviser, Dr. Burnet (afterwards Bishop of Salisbury), to Macclesfield and his troop of two hundred cavaliers on Flemish chargers. There were several organized English regiments that, by arrangement, had been lent to Holland. There was a Swiss legion of fiercely bewhiskered soldiers of fortune, and a band of Swedish knights wearing black cuirasses and cloaks of bearskin. And there was a force of Huguenots, French Protestant exiles recently driven from their own country by Louis' persecution.

It was an international crusade. It embodied the dream of William's life. His banner bore the words, I WILL MAINTAIN THE PROTESTANT RELIGION AND THE

LIBERTIES OF ENGLAND, but it was the first half, more than the second, that inspired his variegated host of volunteers.

He set sail on the day after the vote in the States General, but bad weather drove him back, and it was not until November 1 that his armada finally got under way. First, as a feint, he steered north as though to land in Yorkshire, then tacked and slipped through the Straits of Dover. James' fleet, under Lord Dartmouth, was held powerless in the Thames estuary by the same easterly wind that was blowing the invaders down the English Channel.

William was making for Torbay in Devon, but in the morning haze of November 5 he overshot his objective by several miles. It was a serious mistake. The next harbor along that rocky coast was Plymouth, and Plymouth was held by a man who would probably fight for James. By now, too, Lord Dartmouth might have worked his way out of the Thames and, once around the bend into the Channel, would be coming in hot pursuit. Luckily, at that moment the wind obligingly changed. William was able to swing back into Torbay, and by noon he was ashore at the little fishing village of Brisham.

For a week or two it was touch and go. The West Country people were slow to join him. Their memories were too vivid of the earlier rising against James, three years before, when the Duke of Monmouth's rebellion had ended in the Bloody Assizes before Judge Jeffreys, with wholesale hangings and sentences to slavery in the American plantations.

Like an earlier William at Hastings, the Prince kept his line of retreat open and did not advance far inland during those first doubtful days.

But James was no Saxon Harold, and there was no further likeness between 1066 and 1688. Politicians, generals, whole regiments began to trickle over to the invader. It became a landslide. As William gained confidence and began to push toward London through the southern counties, James found himself deserted by almost everyone—even his daughter Anne. He tried to escape overseas but was recognized by some sailors and turned back. Next to James himself, William was the person most vexed by the sailors' zeal. He meant no personal injury to James, who, besides being his uncle, was his wife's father. If only James had escaped, he would have saved his bacon and at the same time (as another English saying goes) cooked his goose politically. His people would have little use for a king who ran away without making a fight of it.

By Christmas Eve William had reached the little Berkshire town of Abingdon, less than sixty miles from the capital. There, sitting in his billet in the Recorder's house, he received the best Christmas present he could have wished for—the news that James had made a second attempt and this time had managed to leave the country. It was sweet news, more welcome even than those "sweetmeats upon treating the Prince of Orange" which still figure in the Corporation of Abingdon account book, against the sum of £3 5s. 9d.

The "Glorious Revolution" had been accomplished without shedding a drop of blood.

Parliament met in the new year. William was by then installed in London with his troops, but there was endless argument about his exact legal position. Had James II abdicated by fleeing to France? Should there be a regent or a new sovereign? If a new sovereign, who? Obviously not the baby "prince," who was widely believed to be only a cuckoo in the nest. Then Mary, as next in line?

William put his foot down. He would not be regent nor would he play second fiddle to his own wife if she were made queen. "No man can esteem a woman more than I do the Princess," he said bluntly, "but I am so made that I cannot think of holding anything by apron strings. Nor can I think it reasonable to have any share in the government unless it be put in my own person, and that for the term of my life. If you think fit to settle it otherwise, I will not oppose you, but will go back to Holland and meddle no more in your affairs."

Mary wrote from the Hague supporting William. She was angry—as far as so gentle a creature could ever be angry—that the English were not warmer toward her beloved husband. She would not rule without him.

Grumbling, the Lords and Commons made the best of it. Princess Anne agreed to stand aside from second place, so that William, even in his own right, would rank next to Mary. On February 12, Mary arrived from Holland, and for once there were tears in William's eyes as well as her own when they were reunited. On the following day they were waited upon by a Parliamentary delegation in the banqueting hall of the palace, and within a few hours the heralds were proclaiming them joint sovereigns as King William III and Queen Mary II.

So far, so good. But James had meanwhile taken heart. He was not beaten yet. In March came the news that he had landed in Ireland, backed by fifteen French warships and two or three thousand French troops. The Irish were of his own religion, and they were rallying to him. He had entered Dublin. He had advanced into the northern, Protestant counties of Ulster; he was besieging Londonderry.

On April 19, the English Parliament invited William to declare war on Louis whenever he thought fit. For once William almost beamed upon his counselors. "This," he declared triumphantly, "is the first day of my reign!" His dream was taking shape.

He sent troops to Ireland under Marshal Schomberg, a veteran French commander who had been expelled for his Protestant beliefs and who was now a trusted follower of William. But the Irish war dragged on, and after a whole year, during which William was tied to London by State business, he told Parliament he could delay no longer but must go there himself. He appointed a committee of nine to advise Mary while he was away. She would get on well enough, for she understood these tiresome Englishmen better than he did. Except for leaving her, he told Dr. Burnet, "I should enjoy the prospect of being on horseback and under canvas again. For I am sure I am fitter to direct a campaign than to manage your Houses of Lords and Commons!"

On June 14 he landed at Carrickfergus and took over command from old Schomberg. It was obvious to everyone that matters were going to move quickly now and that soon there would be a decision one way or the other. "I haven't come to Ireland to let the grass grow under my feet," he told his men as he issued brisk orders to prepare for action.

Two weeks later the two armies faced each other across the waters of the River Boyne. Occasionally the outpost exchanged a few shots, otherwise all was quiet. William, riding around to inspect the ground, sat down on the riverbank to eat some breakfast. He was noticed and recognized, and two light field guns were brought up by the enemy in time to open fire as William remounted. One shot killed a member of his party, another ricocheted and grazed his shoulder, numbing his sword arm. "No need for any bullet to come nearer," William admitted as the surgeon dressed his wound. Then he climbed stiffly into the saddle again and went on with his rounds until the midsummer dusk began to gather along the water's edge.

The next morning, July 1, dawned fine. William took personal command of his own left wing, all cavalry, and attempted a difficult and dangerous river crossing in the face of the enemy. Here James' Irishmen had a stiffening of French regulars, and it was old Schomberg the Huguenot who rallied the wavering attackers. "Come on, gentlemen!" he cried in French to his fellow exiles. "Yonder are your per-secutors!" The rival bands of Frenchmen went for each other murderously. Schomberg was shot and cut down by sabers. As the attack faltered for the second time, William battled his way across the river with his own Dutch guards and the Irishmen of the Inniskillen regiment. "Men of Inniskillen," he roared, "what will you do for me?" He pointed with his sword—he could scarcely strike with it, because of his wound. The men spurred after him through the bloodstained ford. The defenders broke, and James, watching from the safety of a hilltop, took his place at last at the head of his men—along the Dublin road, to safety.

For William, other battles remained to be fought, but on the continent of Europe. For nearly twelve more years he was to continue his policy of uniting Europe against France. They were to be years of hardship and care. He would never really understand the English, never be popular—but when had he cared much for popularity for its own sake? The English were splendid as comrades on a battlefield, and that was where he wanted them. Their bickerings in Parliament and council chamber he would bear with what patience he could.

He disliked London. The coal smoke stifled him. He lived at Kensington to escape it, and he and Mary began to reconstruct Hampton Court as the kind of country home they both loved. Her sudden death of smallpox, at Christmas 1694, was a tragic blow. "I have never known one single fault in her," he cried out. "No one but I knew her true worth. From being the happiest creature on earth, I am going to be the most miserable!" It was several weeks before he could bear to meet people normally and deal with public business.

Seven years later, one Saturday morning in February, he called for his horse at Kensington and rode off to hunt at Hampton Court. His horse stumbled over a molehill and he was thrown, fracturing his collarbone. It was set by a surgeon and he went home in a carriage, but the jolting of the vehicle displaced the broken bone, and complications set in. On March 8, 1702, William died, and was succeeded by his sister-in-law as Queen Anne.

He was only fifty-one, and his shortish life had been a half century of danger and struggle in which never for one moment had he lost his courage or relaxed his determination. He had not lived to see the success of his plans. Louis remained the great threat to the freedom of Europe, though William had given him some hard knocks, including the recent capture of Namur, which was described as "the greatest humiliation inflicted on Louis in his career of conquest." The great victories—Blenheim and the rest—had been left for Marlborough to win during the next few years. But the foundation for those victories had been laid by the little Dutch general who now slept forever among the kings of England.

THE YEARS BETWEEN

1702-1895

The death of William III came at the opening of one great century for Britain, the eighteenth; the birth of George VI came almost at the close of the next, equally great, century. In that space of time Britain rose steadily to her high-water mark as a world power.

She fought successfully both the old France of Louis, the Sun King, and the revolutionary France of Napoleon. She collected, piece by piece, the vastest empire in history—a subcontinent in India, a half continent in Canada (though she stupidly threw away the chance of another half by her treatment of the American colonists), then a whole continent in Australia, and a global patchwork of islands and other territories. By the latter days of Queen Victoria, before the Empire had begun the opposite process of subdividing into independent dominions, the London government controlled about one fifth of the human race. Yet—as the result of gradual changes starting with the Glorious Revolution of 1688—the actual powers of the sovereign had been reduced. The Prime Minister leading a Parliamentary majority had become the real ruler of the Empire. Kings and queens, though by no means mere figureheads, were evolving into "constitutional monarchs," strictly limited in their political functions, though with many new opportunities to serve their people in other ways.

Meanwhile, the people of the little island itself had made fantastic progress. Those who had not sailed forth to explore and exploit other countries had revolutionized first their farming methods, then their industry. The eighteenth century saw the breeding of better cattle and sheep, the growing of finer crops, than the world had ever seen. The nineteenth century saw Britain leading the rest in the use of steam power—saw her "the workshop of the world." As the century drew to a close, and the life of Victoria with it, Britain seemed secure, powerful, and wealthy beyond belief.

✝✝✝✝✝✝

GEORGE VI: THE

RELUCTANT RULER

It was 1897, the Diamond Jubilee of Queen Victoria. For sixty years that small, iron-willed woman had reigned over an ever-growing empire.

There are many elderly people alive today, in America as well as in Britain, who saw that day in London with their own eyes. Yet to them, looking back, the glittering picture must seem like a fragment of far-off history, almost as remote from us now as the Middle Ages or the Renaissance.

It was a world in which rank and title still cast a spell; a world in which soldiers still wore bright uniforms in battle and charged on horseback with sword and lance; a world of emperors and kings, archdukes and grand dukes, splendid ceremony and freezing etiquette. And Victoria, with her children and grandchildren planted out in every court in Europe, was the supreme matriarch of a system that looked as though it might last a thousand years.

217

That was little more than half a century ago. And already, when older persons recall it, younger ones hardly know what they are talking about.

There is one easy link with our own modern age.

On that Jubilee night, when the crowds crammed the Mall in front of Buckingham Palace (as we have seen them on many later occasions on our movie screens and television), two little boys were among the cluster of royalty acknowledging the cheers from that familiar balcony.

The old queen, their great-grandmother, knew them as David and Bertie.

To us they were to become more familiar under their later titles, the Duke of Windsor and King George VI.

Those little boys, then scarcely visible above the balustrade, link the Victorian world of the dashing Life Guard and the gay hussar with that of the atom bomb.

For the young princes, that visit to the noisy, crowded London of the Jubilee was a thrilling interruption of their quiet country life.

They lived, those two brothers who were destined both to be kings of England, in an ordinary house in Norfolk. The simple entrance hall led to a dining room and two sitting rooms. Upstairs, away from the grownups' bedrooms, they shared a day nursery and a night nursery with their sister Mary, now the Princess Royal. Their windows looked down upon a pond, and sometimes they could watch deer trotting by, small Japanese web-antlered deer that had been imported to graze in the great park of Sandringham.

The house was called York Cottage. Their parents were then the Duke and Duchess of York. The Duke was a bluff, bearded man with the air of a conscientious naval officer—and, indeed, his heart was divided between the navy and the interests of a sporting country gentleman. Long afterwards, in 1935, he was to stand on that same Buckingham Palace balcony and hear the crowds cheering for *his* jubilee, as George V.

Very different in tastes and character was the Duchess. A gracious and beautiful lady, she had other qualities not so common in royal circles then —notably a keen interest in the arts, real knowledge (built up by a remarkable memory), and first-class taste. As Queen Mary she lived to a great age, dying in 1953, loved and respected on both sides of the Atlantic.

Bertie—or Albert more formally ("George" was merely his official name when he became king)— was very much the product of these home surroundings and the child of these parents, whereas his elder brother David was a natural rebel, as can be seen from his own book, *A King's Story*. It was Bertie who, like his father, loved the simple country life of Sandringham and the disciplined existence of a naval officer, but in him his father's rougher manner was softened with some of his mother's gentler and more charming qualities.

David—who was later to give up a throne for the woman he loved—had much more in common with his grandparents, who lived at the big house a quarter of a mile away across the park. His grandfather was then Prince of Wales but was soon to succeed Victoria as King Edward VII. He was a gay, easy-going man who loved the social round of the London season, the great country houses of England, and the fashionable pleasure resorts of the Continent. His wife was the Danish princess Alexandra, amusing, kittenish, without any sense of time, so that she was almost too late for her own coronation.

For, at last, Victoria died.

Bertie was just five—he had been born at York Cottage on December 14, 1895, and the old Queen died in January, 1901. The little princes were in bed with the measles, but they recovered in time to watch the pageantry of her funeral. Almost immediately afterwards the Duke and Duchess set out on a world tour, and for eight months the children stayed with their grandparents, the new King and Queen. Most grandparents spoil children, if given half a chance. Edward and Alexandra were no exception. Nursery routine and lessons were swept aside with an indulgent wave of the King's cigar, and the Queen in any case was never conscious of the clock. The three children ran wild, sometimes at Osborne in the Isle of Wight, sometimes at Balmoral in the Scottish Highlands, but mostly at the big house at Sandringham.

Sandringham was a boy's paradise. Bertie grew to love it as his brother never did. There were miles of woodland, oak and pine and yew. There were vast expanses of feathery bracken, and beyond it stretched the tidal marshes of the North Sea. There were trees to climb, horses to ride, and a flat-bottomed boat to navigate on the little lake in front of York Cottage.

Of course, once the Duke and Duchess came home, life was more ordered. The Duke believed sternly in discipline. If the children were naughty, they were summoned to their father's den—and they went in fear and trembling, for when angry he was like a ship's captain raging on his quarterdeck.

The boys were put in the charge of men from an early age. They had a nursery footman named Finch, a picturesque character whose father had served the famous Duke of Wellington. There was nothing servile about Finch. He was tough with the small boys when toughness was required. He brought them up in the way they were to go.

As they grew too old for a governess, they were given a tutor, Mr. Hansell—a "tall, gaunt, solemn stranger with a large mustache" was David's first impression of him. He was a typical public school and Oxford man of those days, only moderately intellectual, a good footballer, golfer, and shot, interested in old churches but not in religion, a gentleman, a bachelor, a pipe smoker, and a wearer of comfortable tweeds.

Mr. Hansell's foreign languages were not of the standard needed for teaching princes, who really need French and German conversation, if only to understand visiting relatives; so other tutors were added for special subjects, and weekly reports were sent to the boys' father. In one of these, the German tutor, Professor Oswald, described Bertie as *"inattentive and playful."*

"What do you mean, 'playful'?" growled the Duke.

"When I scold him," said the unhappy tutor, "he just pulls my beard!"

Bertie had his mischievous moments. Later, as a naval cadet, he was to be punished with his classmates for setting off fireworks in the lavatories. But in general he was a conscientious boy, not in trouble so often as David was.

One of the pleasantest hours in the day was just after tea, which the boys and their sister always spent with their mother. She lay relaxed on a sofa, talking or reading to them before she went to dress for the evening. Sometimes she taught them songs —not only the old English songs but American favorites such as "Swanee River" and "Camptown Races." She did not believe in idle fingers—to the end of her long life she used to do needlework while a lady in waiting read to her—and the young princes, as well as Princess Mary, had to do simple knitting as they listened.

Bertie never forgot those happy after-tea sessions with his mother. He learned then that public personages, however full their daily round may be, must somehow find time also to be good parents. In later years, when he had children of his own, the present Queen Elizabeth and Princess Margaret, he always made time to play with them and enter into their interests. His daughter has carried on the tradition: though duty often takes Queen Elizabeth away from her children, whenever possible she devotes that regular hour to Prince Charles and Princess Anne.

It was an important element in the forming of Bertie's character and outlook. Kings and queens in bygone centuries had not usually spent so much time with their children. Royal history is full of feuds between fathers and sons, husbands and wives; and palaces do not always provide good examples of happy family life. There was misunderstanding between Queen Victoria and her eldest son, and again between George V (to a lesser extent) and the Duke of Windsor. But Bertie, the quieter, shyer, younger brother, fitted more easily into his parents' ways. Year by year he developed the character that one day (though he never suspected it) would equip him to carry on their work.

Most of the year was spent at Sandringham. It was the one royal home that had never been shadowed by the presence of Queen Victoria, with her morbid passion for mourning not only her long-dead husband but every departed pet animal or other reminder of vanished happiness. Sandringham had begun as gay Grandfather's own country estate. It has remained, ever since, the traditional family meeting place for Christmas and other occasions.

In the early summer, though, the children left Sandringham for the London "season," though they were as yet too young to share in the numerous balls and dinner parties and similar fashionable festivities. The "season" then had a brilliance and sparkle

now lost forever. The nobility all kept town houses
with hosts of servants. Each night the streets and
squares were gay with music floating from open windows. Red carpets stretched across the sidewalks to
the never-ending stream of carriages. The new King
and Queen were brightening society after the long
reign of an anything but "merry widow." The Ed-
wardian era came like a brief Indian summer tagged
onto the safe and prosperous era of Victoria. The
calendar might show the twentieth century, but
historically it was more like a postscript to the nineteenth.

Change was on the way, but Mr. Hansell and
Finch and the others were not seriously concerned,
and the young princes grew up with little forebod-
ing of the future.

Father's cousin, the German Emperor, might
make silly speeches, which annoyed Grandfather
and made him anxious for a closer friendship between Britain and France, the Entente Cordiale.
. . . The Japanese might surprise (and rather delight) the world by sinking the Russian fleet and
beating the Russian armies in the Far East. . . .
The newly formed Labour Party might win its first
big success (fifty-one seats in the sensational election of 1906), and determined women, calling
themselves "suffragettes," might be demanding
votes and doing extraordinary things to win public-
ity for their cause: attacking policemen, smashing
windows, and chaining themselves to the railings
outside the Prime Minister's house in Downing

Street. . . . Shabby-looking foreigners might be meeting in the drabber parts of London to plan the Bolshevik Revolution for Russia. . . .

But the life of the little princes went on as usual —the "season" in "Town," then the Royal Ascot races, then a holiday alone with Mamma at Frogmore, close to Windsor Castle, then to Scotland with her to join Papa for his autumn deer stalking, and back to Sandringham for Papa to shoot pheasant and for everyone else to look forward to Christmas.

Younger brothers were born at intervals—Henry, the present Duke of Gloucester, and George, the late Duke of Kent, killed in an air crash while on active service in the Second World War, and John, who died young. David and Bertie had a special link as the two eldest, but their temperaments were very different and they never teamed up in any special partnership dividing them from the others.

They both went to the Naval Training College at Osborne. Papa did not approve of ordinary schools for princes, but he approved of the Navy. Was it not the "senior service," always more highly honored in Britain than the Army? Was it not the career he had always hankered after himself?

"Treat him as a cadet," he ordered Bertie's tutor, "and make him realize his responsibilities."

Bertie, then just entering his teens, asked for nothing more. "I am a midshipman," he would remind anyone who tried to treat him as a prince. When, at fifteen, he moved over to the Naval College at Dartmouth in Devon (that lovely landlocked haven familiar to so many American servicemen during the months of preparation for D-Day), it was the same story.

"He never once asked for a favor, all the time he was at Dartmouth," testified one officer, "nor did he once use his position to gain a favor for anyone else."

He was not brilliant and he was not physically strong. Already he was hampered by the poor health that dogged him off and on throughout his life. He was shy and diffident, troubled by a hesitation in his speech that was later to make public appearances an ordeal. But—to quote another officer —"he had a tremendous lot of guts. You knew instinctively that he would never let you down." He battled against his weaknesses. He went through the toughest training, though during those years he had influenza, pneumonia, and continual pains that were climaxed, a little later, in appendicitis. He accepted the routine and the discipline more willingly than David did. One of his officers forecast that in time, despite his disadvantages, he would outstrip his elder brother.

Meanwhile, just before he moved to Dartmouth after his fifteenth birthday, Papa had come to the throne as King George V. David was Prince of Wales now, and Bertie next in the line of succession. That, of course, meant nothing. David, so charming and self-confident and popular, would be sure to marry. Barring some cruel mischance within the next few years, there was not the faintest possibility (the shy young cadet told himself thankfully) that he would ever have to take on the awful responsibility of being king. David, and David's sons after him, would take care of all that. Bertie could give his mind to the ships and the sea he was beginning to love.

At seventeen he was posted to H.M.S. *Cumberland* and went off on a cruise to Canada and the West Indies. As any other boy would have done, he enjoyed the adventure of seeing strange lands and tropical seas for the first time and of serving, as a newly fledged naval officer, in his very first ship. But there was something else he had to do for the first time, and this he did not enjoy so much. He had to make a formal public appearance and deliver a speech.

The *Cumberland* had cast anchor at Kingstown, Jamaica. There was a new wing to be opened at the Yacht Club. What more fitting opener than His Royal Highness Prince Albert? Battling with his nerves, the boy learned his speech by heart and took his stand on the decorated platform. The crowd was tremendous. The body of the hall was packed in front of him, the platform behind him was solid with humanity—and all the people pressing most closely around him appeared to be the young ladies of the island, each eager to boast afterwards how near she had stood to "a real live prince."

As he began to speak, he was acutely conscious that he was being poked in the back or behind the knees and that loyal fingers were tweaking his trouser legs. Behind his own voice, struggling to bring out the fine formal phrases he had memorized, he

caught an undertone of giggles and whispered in-
quiries:

"Have you touched him?"

"Yes. Have you?"

"Yes, three times!"

"I've touched him four!"

He got through his speech. He was that sort of
boy.

After a holiday with his family in the Highlands,
the Prince was posted to another warship, the
Collingwood, and served with the Mediterranean
Fleet, as later his son-in-law, the Duke of Edinburgh, was to do.

By now the world was drifting very close to the
first Great War of 1914, but to most ordinary people the danger was hidden. There was none of that
"crisis atmosphere" that filled the years before
1939. Some believed that a war between civilized
nations had become impossible; others thought
that, if it came, it would be short and romantic; few
had the power to imagine what it would really be
like.

Europe drifted on toward disaster, as a pleasure
boat races along on the smooth, unruffled water
above the unseen weir. In a few hot summer days in
1914 nation after nation plunged over the edge into
tragedy.

The Austro-Hungarian Empire threatened its
small neighbor Serbia, now part of Yugoslavia.

The Russian Empire mustered its ill-equipped
hosts to support the Serbians.

The Kaiser, the German Emperor, mobilized his army, the most efficient fighting machine in Europe, to support the Austrians.

France was bound by alliance to Russia. The French were called up in readiness to fight the hated Germans, who had beaten them and captured Paris only forty-three years before.

Britain came into it when the Kaiser sent his troops through the territory of neutral Belgium, for Britain had guaranteed the independence of Belgium. On August 4, war was declared on Germany.

It proved to be mainly a land war, and Prince Albert saw little excitement. The British Navy was overwhelmingly strong: though the Kaiser had built up a big fleet, he did not dare risk it on the high seas. Except for one famous occasion, the Battle of Jutland, the Germans confined their efforts to submarine warfare, mine laying, and light cruiser raids. The callous sinking of the liner *Lusitania* by a German submarine brought vigorous protests from Washington, and for a time the Germans adopted different tactics. But when they resumed unrestricted submarine warfare, the United States came into the war as an associate of France and Great Britain.

Most of the time, therefore, the Prince was tied to the dreary northern naval base of Scapa Flow, at the remotest tip of Scotland, hoping that one day the German High Seas Fleet would venture forth from its den and fight. It was nearly two years before the chance came, at the end of May, 1916. News came that the Germans had put to sea, and the British Grand Fleet of fifty-one warships steamed out to engage them.

The battle that followed was fought at long range and did not give the British the glorious victory they had hoped for. True, the Germans turned and fled to the safety of their bases, from which they never came out again except to surrender, two and a half years later. But the British losses were the heavier, and many people blamed the British admiral, Jellicoe, for not pressing the pursuit more closely. Probably he was right to be cautious. If he had risked piling up his ships on the German mine fields, he might have lost Britain the command of the seas. As Sir Winston Churchill remarked, "Jellicoe was the only man on either side who could have lost the war in an afternoon."

Meanwhile, the Prince described his own experiences in a letter to his former tutor:

"The Jutland battle was a great thing to have been in, and it certainly was different from what I expected. We, of course, in the *Collingwood,* saw a great deal more than some of the other ships and we fired more than they did. We were not hit at all, which was very lucky, though we were straddled several times. One shell dropped over the foc's'le, missing us by inches. I was in the fore turret, second in command. During some of it, I was sitting on the top when they straddled us. I didn't remain up very long after that. The men were quite marvellous. Just as cheery as usual, and worked like demons."

Twenty years later, when he drove to Buckingham Palace to take up his residence as King, he carried

with him, as talisman, the flag the *Collingwood* had
flown on that exciting day.

By the last year of the war, aircraft had become so
important that a new service was formed, distinct
from the Navy and the Army, and the Prince was appointed to be its royal figurehead. Somewhat reluctantly, he changed the uniform of a naval lieutenant
for that of the Royal Air Force.

It was typical of his character that he quickly
worked up plenty of interest and enthusiasm for the
new work laid upon him. Typical, too, that he felt
ashamed to wear the winged badge of a pilot when
in fact he could not fly a plane. Over and over again
he begged for permission to train as a pilot; both his
father and the Government agreed that, being next
to the Prince of Wales in line for the throne, he must
not risk his life in the air. At last, a month or
two after the Germans collapsed and asked for
peace, he won his point. He trained and was tested
in the ordinary way, and earned the right to wear
his "wings" like any other aviator. It was a proud
day. It is not often that royalty gets the chance to
prove its skill—but there are no two ways about pi-
loting a plane. Either one can or one cannot. The
Prince could.

Now, with the war over, there was a chance to
learn other things. David was sent to Oxford, Bertie
to Cambridge. He lived in a small house there and
cycled to lectures in the various colleges. Here, once
again, he insisted on being treated like other young
men. When the servants irritated him by tagging on

his title to the end of every sentence, he made a rule of his own:

"You may call me 'Your Royal Highness' once a day, and then no more. I'm sick of it!"

He was subject to the same university discipline as the other students. When caught smoking in the streets (he was now twenty-four), he was fined the traditional sum of six shillings and eightpence, this strange amount representing half the medieval coin called a mark.

While still a Cambridge undergraduate, Bertie began to take on his share of public duties.

The British royal family suffers from an immense burden of these. Some, such as the opening of Parliament, the regular conferences with Government leaders, and the signing of innumerable papers, can be done only by the reigning king or queen. But there are countless other functions—the launching of new ships, the opening of hospitals, the inspection of regiments, the visiting of factories, mines, schools, exhibitions, and sporting events—with which other members of the family are expected to lend a hand.

"We are not a family," the Prince lamented years later, only half jokingly, "we are a firm."

It was the burden of these duties, never shirked and always conscientiously performed, that was later to shorten his life.

Meanwhile, though he still found public speaking an ordeal, he was proving himself, even to the satisfaction of his critical father. Before he left Cambridge he received the good news that the King had created him Duke of York. "Duke," to an American ear, may sound lower than "prince," but in fact it was a promotion. In Britain "prince" (except "Prince of Wales") only means the son of a sovereign. To be a royal duke is to hold a title of one's own. Thus, to be Duke of Edinburgh meant new honor for Prince Philip, and "Duke of Cornwall" spelled advancement for young Prince Charles.

When Bertie was made Duke of York (as his father had once been before him) he knew that he had passed another test. He had won his wings again, but in a different sense.

During the following years he did not often make the newspaper headlines in a big way. He was tireless in his public duties, but he was almost always overshadowed by the more glamorous personality of David. It was David who, as Prince of Wales, toured the world as a kind of special ambassador; David who galloped furiously after the foxhounds, rode in steeplechases (and not seldom came off); David who owned a ranch in Canada and was the darling of America; David whom every sentimental girl dreamed of marrying.

Only once did the younger brother take the limelight. That was when, on a showery April day, he drove to Westminster Abbey to marry Lady Elizabeth Bowes-Lyon. He was twenty-seven; she was twenty-two, a Scottish girl brought up in Macbeth's castle of Glamis, daughter of the Earl of Strathmore and descended from the ancient kings of Scotland. They made a striking couple, the bridegroom tall and lean in his brilliant uniform, the bride pretty and charming rather than classically beautiful, but already possessed of that natural grace that she still wears as the Queen Mother. It was the first royal wedding in the Abbey since Richard of Bordeaux's marriage to Anne of Bohemia in the Middle Ages. It was small wonder that London went wild that day and that the young Duke shared the headlines with his bride.

There was one other thing that caught the imagination during that period—his idea of "the Duke of York's Camp."

This was an annual summer camp for four hundred boys, half of them from factories and mines, half from the great schools of the kingdom. They came as his guests, and each year he spent a day with them, sharing their games and fireside singsongs. He would never go for more than one day. He knew that, try as he might to sink himself into the crowd, no one could ever quite forget that he was the King's son. He did not want to spoil the carefree, natural atmosphere of the camp, in which class distinctions were laid aside and the boys from Eton and Harrow made friends with boys from the coal face and the conveyor belt.

The idea was taken up and extended by others, both in England and in the Dominions. Altogether many thousands of boys took part in this democratic experiment.

So the years passed, the nineteen-twenties merging into the nineteen-thirties. History was made. Dictators arose, casting giant shadows across the

world—Mussolini in Fascist Italy, Stalin in Commu-
nist Russia, Hitler in Nazi Germany. There was a
great trade depression in America, the backwash of
which swept over other countries, swelling the millions of unemployed and overthrowing governments, including the British Labour government of
1931. History was made, but not by the Duke. He
went on quietly and unassumingly, like any other
citizen, fulfilling his duties and enjoying a happy
family life. Two daughters had been born, the present Queen Elizabeth in 1926 and, four years later,
Princess Margaret, then always referred to as Margaret Rose.

David was still unmarried, and this fact was a considerable worry to the aging King. Very soon, in
1935, George V would celebrate the Silver Jubilee
of his reign. He could not live forever. Soon David
would be king. Who then would be queen?

It was possible, of course, to have a bachelor king,
but not desirable. No queen would certainly be better than the wrong queen. It was a heavy responsibility, calling for special qualities. The Queen of
England was the first lady not only in Britain but in
the British Empire. She must be able, naturally and
without effort or question, to command the respect
of every subject, rich or poor, white or colored, ancient aristocrat or workingman, Roman Catholic,
Protestant, Jew, Moslem, or Hindu.

David, now entering his forties, showed no sign
of choosing such a wife to share his destiny.

None of his women friends looked like a future
Queen of England. Indeed—much to his father's

concern—David's particular friend was an American woman who was married, had divorced a previous husband, and seemed likely to apply for a divorce again. There was nothing against the woman's own character, there was nothing against David's liking for Americans, but divorce in Britain meant something different from what it did in the United States. For one thing, it carried more of a suggestion of disgrace (which was unfair to the innocent partner), simply because British divorces were granted only for serious and shameful reasons. Secondly, millions of people—all Roman Catholics and very many members of the Church of England—believed that no divorce court could really destroy a religious sacrament, and so, logically, no subsequent marriage by a divorced person was a marriage at all in the eyes of God.

Whether or not this point of view is right might be a good subject for argument. But a Queen of England must not be a subject for argument. She must unite people, not divide them. And any queen with a former husband still alive would most certainly divide the Empire most violently. Many of her people would be unable to look upon her as their king's lawful wife, or his children as lawful heirs to the throne. That question had caused quite enough trouble in the far-off days of Henry VIII.

The matter did not come to a head in the old King's lifetime, but it certainly clouded his happiness during that last summer of his Silver Jubilee. The Duke of York must have known of it, though the general public was blissfully ignorant. Outside smart society, the name of Mrs. Simpson (as she then was) remained quite unknown.

In January, 1936, George V died. David was at once proclaimed King, taking the title of Edward VIII. For some strange reason, modern kings, like popes, very often take quite different names from those they bear in private company. It is a little confusing for readers of their biographies.

The new monarch continued his friendship with Mrs. Simpson, who was now applying for a British divorce from her husband. Still the British public had no knowledge of the matter. There was no official censorship, but all the newspapers privately agreed together, from patriotic motives, to publish nothing. So far it was only a private and perfectly respectable friendship, but gossip might harm the King. The wholesale newspaper firms joined in the conspiracy of silence. Imported American magazines were inspected for photographs and articles dealing too freely with the question, and either they were not distributed or the offending items were cut out.

The secret was kept until the autumn, though it had been gradually leaking out to more and more people who were on the fringe of court society or were told by friends writing from abroad. Still, when the story finally broke—through an outspoken sermon preached by a bishop—ninety-nine per cent of the population was taken completely by surprise.

There were a few days of agitated crisis. Unmuzzled, the press poured out its views and speculations. Should the King marry the woman he loved? If she could not be Queen, could she not just be his wife, as a private citizen, by a "morganatic" marriage? Some newspapers and public leaders (including Winston Churchill) backed the King. The majority, led by the National Government of Stanley Baldwin and the Archbishop of Canterbury, and supported by the various governments of the Empire overseas, were resolute that no marriage of any kind must take place between the King and Mrs. Simpson.

In the midst of the crisis David summoned his brother to Fort Belvedere, the quaint little mock-Gothic, battlemented house that he had turned into his private retreat six miles from Windsor Castle across the Great Park.

Astounded, Bertie listened to David's decision. David was prepared to give up everything. He was going to marry Mrs. Simpson when her divorce was granted. If he could not do so as King, he would stop being King.

That meant the crown must pass to Bertie. The shy brother—the man who hated fuss and limelight, who, in his own words, "was not palace-minded"— must be condemned for life to the burden of king-ship. And not only himself condemned, but his heir after him. Probably (since there was still no son) that meant the carefree ten-year-old Elizabeth.

He said little at the time. True to character, he thought things over quietly, and a few days later sent his brother a note. "I long for you to be happy. I am sure that whatever you decide will be in the best interests of the country and the Empire." A few more days passed, the King holding aloof from his family until the issue was finally decided. Then all the brothers were summoned to the Fort to sign, in order of seniority, the various copies of the Abdication which were to be sent to each imperial capital across the world.

No English king had ever really abdicated before. James II had fled the country, but he had never renounced the throne. Richard II had gone through a ceremony of abdication, but the circumstances had been suspicious and his murder had followed quickly afterwards. Only Edward VIII was giving up an empire by his own choice.

That evening the two brothers had a last talk. "You're not going to find this a difficult job at all," said the elder. "You know all the ropes. And you've almost overcome that slight hesitation in your speech."

The Duke raised a minor query, but one that had to be settled at once. What should David be called when he ceased to be King? He could not be Prince of Wales again. It was agreed that the new sovereign's very first act should be to create the ex-King Duke of Windsor.

There was a farewell family dinner that night at Royal Lodge, Windsor. Queen Mary and the Princess Royal joined the men. After the meal, David went over to the Castle alone, to broadcast a statement to the people. Bertie stayed with the others around the radio and heard his brother's voice come over the air:

"At long last I am able to say a few words of my own. . . . A few hours ago I discharged my last duty as King and Emperor, and, now I have been succeeded by my brother, the Duke of York, my first words must be to declare my allegiance to him. . . ."

It was soon over. They switched off. In a few minutes David was back. His mother and sister left, the brothers stayed for a last drink together. David, of course, must leave the country. So long as he stayed, people would feel that they had two kings at once. The destroyer *Fury* was already standing by at Portsmouth, to carry him across the Channel to France.

The glasses were emptied, the last words spoken. They went to the door to see him off. But this time it was David, as the subject, who bowed to his younger brother as the new King. And the Duke of Kent, youngest of them all, shook his head sorrowfully and muttered fiercely:

"It isn't possible! It isn't happening!"

But it was. It was no dream. Very soon the heralds would be proclaiming Bertie as King George VI.

There were many persons at the time who believed that the English monarchy could never recover its dignity and glamour after the abdication. It was as though the curtain had been snatched aside, revealing to the common gaze some inner shrine. Or as if, in a stage play, the popular star had been replaced by an understudy.

It is strange now to look back, and hard to believe. The remarkable recovery of the British royal family is due to the restraint and good taste of all those personally concerned, not excluding the Duke of Windsor and the woman he soon afterward made his Duchess.

But most of all it was due to the character of the new King, the help given him by his wife (in whom England found a Queen to satisfy the most critical Prime Minister or Archbishop of Canterbury), and the dignified background support of his mother, the recently widowed Queen Mary, who had come through a tragic twelve months with unwavering self-control.

With his usual dislike of fuss, the new King let the original date stand for the coronation, and quick changes were made so that he could be crowned in his brother's stead on May 12, 1937. Five million cheering people crammed the London streets that day. Crowned and cloaked in ermine, a slender figure in red and white and gold, George VI looked down from that Buckingham Palace balcony on which he had first stood with Queen Victoria forty years before. With him, in their crowns and coronets, stood his wife and his mother and the two eager, excited little girls.

Little more than two years of peace remained to Britain. This time the approaching shadow loomed for all to see. The Japanese were carving up China. Mussolini had conquered Abyssinia. Hitler was howling against the Jews, the Czechs, the Russians. The western democracies began, almost too late, to arm for their own defense.

Against this lowering background the bright ceremonies of royalty had to go on as usual. Quickly, painstakingly, the King mastered his new duties, gained in confidence. Helped by the Queen, he improved his public speaking and was able to make the annual Christmas broadcasts to his people all over the world, just as his father had done.

In May and June, 1939, he and the Queen made a six-thousand-mile tour of Canada, right across to British Columbia and the Pacific, and found time for an all-too-brief visit to the United States. New York gave them a characteristic welcome with bands and cheering crowds and ticker tape snowing from the upper windows. Washington was more formal—until President Roosevelt, with insight and sympathy, swept them off to the peace of Hyde Park. "They are coming away for a quiet week end with me," he announced. "I'll put the King into an old pair of flannels and just drive him about in my old Ford." He could have done nothing kinder. George VI liked America. Though he spent little time in the States, he had many American tastes, including a liking for the humor of Danny Kaye.

Five weeks after he landed home at Southampton, Hitler invaded Poland. History repeated itself. Just a quarter of a century before, it had been Belgium. Again Britain called on the Germans to halt their armies. Again, on their contemptuous refusal, Britain declared war.

After that, history did not repeat itself—much— and struck out on a new, more terrible line. In less than twelve months Hitler and his junior partner, Mussolini, held the whole continent of Europe, west of Russia, except for a few small pockets that it suited them better to leave as neutral.

Britain stood alone, except for her distant dominions and colonies and the small but useful numbers of Frenchmen, Poles, Norwegians, and other Europeans who had escaped from the mainland. America was neutral, though friendly and helpful, and did not come in until the Japanese attack on Pearl Harbor. Russia was neutral, but unfriendly and unhelpful, until she became an ally overnight when Hitler launched a surprise invasion across her borders. Until then, Britain was alone, on the fringe of a conquered Europe, just as she had been in the age of Napoleon. But this time she was in far more mortal danger, for this was the age of the bomber, the Fifth Column of traitors, the parachutist, and the panzer brigade.

The King and the Government knew, far more vividly than the people, the full weakness of the defending forces. He was asked to consider moving to Canada, or at least to send the princesses there, as many parents had sent their children. He refused. The royal family would take its chance with all the other families who could not possibly get away.

He worked harder than ever now, though his public appearances could never be announced beforehand, lest the German bombers should pinpoint the spot. He was continually inspecting troops, naval units, airfields, factories—and, above all, the people bombed out of their homes in air raids. He was amid the smoking ruins of Coventry within a few hours of the savage attack that made that city famous throughout the world.

How the people felt about him is expressed in this letter sent to a London newspaper years afterward:

"We, the ordinary working-class people, loved our King dearly. Somehow he seemed to get deeper into our hearts than any of the others we've had, and we don't want any of the great men to keep on telling *us* what a good king *he* was. We've known that all along. Didn't he stop with us through all the bombing when he could have gone to safety, as everyone hoped he would? Maybe it was that alone that *got us* more than anything else. Remember that morning in the East End, after one of the worst raids, when he brought the Queen with him, and walked among the ruin and rubble, talking to anyone, comforting and consoling. Then that rough chap who couldn't hold himself any longer burst out with, 'You're a *good* King, sir!' He turned (God bless him) and he didn't stammer then, and said, 'And you're a *good* people!'"

Buckingham Palace was bombed several times. It was one of the first buildings in London to receive a direct hit. Later it was hit three separate times within a week. When not touring, the King spent his days working at the Palace and went down to Windsor to sleep, except when he worked so late that he had to remain in London overnight. Both he and the Queen were in the building when a German dive bomber scattered five bombs on and around it.

As the tide of war turned in Britain's favor, thanks to the entry of America and the tremendous losses suffered by the Germans on the Russian front, he paid various journeys to visit his troops in the field. In June, 1943, he flew to North Africa and was entertained by the brilliant British commander, Montgomery, at his famous caravan headquarters in the western desert. He went on to the beleaguered island of Malta, which, though pounded by enemy bombers from the nearby mainland of Italy, guarded the vital Mediterranean sea route from Gibraltar to the Suez Canal.

The next year, as D-Day approached, he was one of the few people who knew the actual invasion date selected by General (later President) Eisenhower. He was in constant touch with Winston Churchill by secret telephone, and they lunched together each week so that they could have a full discussion on what was happening. Nine days after D-Day, the King himself landed on the Normandy beaches and saw for himself the perilous little bridgehead that had been secured for the liberation of Europe. A few weeks later he was in Italy with the troops who were driving up from the south as the other claw of the pincers that were grasping at victory. It was in Italy that, hearing that many G.I.s wanted to get their own snapshots of the British King, he arranged to meet a crowd of them and pose for their cameras.

Within a year the war in Europe was won. Once again, on V-E Day, May 8, 1945, the roadway in front of the palace was solid with cheering people, and once again the historic balcony was lined with smiling, waving royalty—the King in his favorite uniform as a naval officer, Princess Elizabeth in the khaki of a woman army lieutenant, and the Prime Minister, Winston Churchill, beaming like a benevolent bulldog in the place where he deserved to be, between the King and the Queen, in the middle of their family.

A few months later President Truman was hurrying back to America from a conference in Berlin. There was no time for him to visit London. The King had never stood on ceremony, and though the head of the State normally stays at home and expects his visitors to come to him, he made the journey down to Plymouth Sound so that he could meet President Truman before he sailed out of the Channel into the Atlantic. It was a symbolic encounter —King and President chatting warmly as friends, and a British band playing "The Star-Spangled Banner" not a mile from the stone which commemorates the sailing of the *Mayflower*.

Victory was won now all over the globe, for Japan surrendered a few months after Germany. But for the King there was little hope of rest.

Britain, bomb-shattered, impoverished, and thoroughly disorganized for peacetime living by six years of all-out war effort, faced desperate problems. Millions of houses to be built or repaired, millions of fighting men to be got back into civilian life, shortages of food, clothing, paper, books, coal, electricity, and every normal necessity, India and Burma and Ceylon and Palestine all demanding their independence. . . . Though it was the business of the Government to decide on policies, the King had to know and understand all that was going on. He could not escape his share of the burden. As for public appearances and royal tours, never had they been so badly needed. The people were worn out by years of hardship. They needed cheering after the long age of dark streets and blacked-out windows. They wanted to come out into the open, to switch on all the lights, to wave their flags and let off their fireworks. It was in that spirit that they undertook the Festival of Britain, which the King opened from the steps of St. Paul's Cathedral in 1950.

It is no exaggeration to say that the King killed himself by his devotion to duty in those seven years following the war. In 1947 he had visited South Africa, the first reigning sovereign to do so; and in 1948 he was planning a tour of Australia and New Zealand when his doctors stepped in and insisted that he should not only cancel the tour but take twelve months' rest from public ceremonies. But in actual fact, nothing like so long a rest was taken. Within a few months the King was holding an investiture at the palace—and, needless to say, the "paper work," the signing of innumerable documents and the discussion of business with countless officials, had never been relaxed at all. In March he had an operation on his right leg, and soon he was undertaking the full burden of his public appearances once more.

There was much private happiness in these years.

He saw his elder daughter married, saw the birth of two grandchildren, Prince Charles and Princess Anne. His wife was a tower of strength. His mother was still alive, serene and splendid, the grand old lady of England.

In 1951 he was gravely ill again. He recovered, and only a few people knew that he could never be really well again, that—to quote the moving words of Winston Churchill broadcasting on the day after his death—"he endured his life hanging by a thread from day to day . . . all the time cheerful and un-daunted—stricken in body but quite undisturbed and even unaffected in spirit. During these last months the King walked with death, as if death were a companion, an acquaintance whom he rec-ognized and did not fear. In the end death came as a friend; and after a happy day of sunshine and sport, and after 'good night' to those who loved him best, he fell asleep as every man or woman who strives to fear God and nothing else in the world may hope to do."

The end came at Sandringham, the country home where he was born and where he had always been happiest. February 5, 1952, was a pleasant winter's day in the Norfolk woods. The King walked a little and shot in the game coverts where that great sportsman, his father, had first taught him to hold a gun. He went home to tea, spent a fireside evening with his family—except for Princess Elizabeth, who was far away in East Africa, starting the tour he himself had had to cancel—and went early to bed. About seven o'clock the next morning his valet went to call him. He seemed to be sleeping peacefully, but at a second glance the valet saw that he would never wake again.

His tour of duty was over. Release had come to the reluctant King.